GOVERNING PARADOXES OF RESTORATIVE JUSTICE

GOVERNING PARADOXES OF RESTORATIVE JUSTICE

George Pavlich

London • Sydney • Portland, Oregon

First published in Great Britain 2005 by
GlassHouse Press, The Glass House,
Wharton Street, London WC1X 9PX, United Kingdom
Telephone: + 44 (0)20 7278 8000   Facsimile: + 44 (0)20 7278 8080
Email: info@cavendishpublishing.com
Website: www.cavendishpublishing.com

Published in the United States by Cavendish Publishing
c/o International Specialized Book Services,
5824 NE Hassalo Street, Portland,
Oregon 97213-3644, USA

Published in Australia by The GlassHouse Press,
45 Beach Street, Coogee, NSW 2034, Australia
Telephone: + 61 (2)9664 0909   Facsimile: +61 (2)9664 5420
Email: info@cavendishpublishing.com.au
Website: www.cavendishpublishing.com.au

© George Pavlich 2005

British Library Cataloguing in Publication Data
Pavlich, George C (George Clifford), 1960–
The governing paradoxes of restorative justice
1 Restorative justice
I Title
364.6'8

Library of Congress Cataloguing in Publication Data
Data available

ISBN 1-90438-519-2
ISBN 978-1-904-38519-6

1 3 5 7 9 10 8 6 4 2

Printed and bound in Great Britain

For Pav and Tally

Acknowledgments

Although at times an isolated pursuit, writing is also the product of many influences that saturate the narratives eventually countersigned as a text. Many are those who have helped to move the project from loose ideas to a recurrently reworked, though never quite finished, manuscript. Although too many to name here, I would like to thank all those friends and colleagues who have taken the time to discuss, comment on or otherwise assist with this work – including Curtis Clark, Kathy Daly, Lois Harder, Myra Hird, Bryan Hogeveen, Greg McLennan, Pat O'Malley, Wes Pue, Declan Roche, Ros Sydie, Andrew Woolford and Deena Workum. Bob Ratner's penetrating questioning at an early stage of the project helped to clarify many aspects of the overall argument, while Kit Carson helped me to grapple with vexing questions of crime and community.

I should like also to acknowledge the University of Alberta for granting me sabbatical leave, and colleagues at the School of Law at Birkbeck College, University of London, for providing such a conducive, collegial and vibrant intellectual setting for completing much of the book. I am especially grateful to Peter Fitzpatrick for his support, inspiring amity, incisive discussions and excellent advice on this book at a crucial stage of its development. Beverley Brown of the GlassHouse Press also deserves a special note of thanks – she went beyond the call of editorial duty in providing such supportive, assiduous and thoughtfully nuanced commentaries on an earlier draft of what follows.

Finally, Carla and Seth deserve a special note of thanks for putting up with my odd hours, absences and general distractions. I have written once before and do not mind repeating it here: they tangibly incarnate what makes this all worthwhile. For that, I am afraid, there is simply no adequate thanks.

Contents

Acknowledgments		*vii*
1	**Tracing Auspices of Restorative Justice**	1
2	**Healing Crime's Harm**	25
3	**Victims of Restorative Governmentalities**	43
4	**Responsible Offenders**	65
5	**The State of Restored Communities**	83
6	**Justice Anew?**	105
Bibliography		121
Index		139

Chapter I
Tracing Auspices of Restorative Justice

For centuries, justice has been figured through the symbol of a blindfolded Themis. She bears the scales of impartiality in one hand and a sword of power in the other, evoking this allegorical message: justice is possible when a neutral judge calculates a fair balance of accounts to arrive at decisions backed by the force of a sovereign power. The detached fairness of equally considered, yet enforced, judgments provides a basic rationale for the machinations of modern courtrooms and associated legal measures. Despite this rationale's dominance in criminal matters, the past few decades have witnessed calls for a return to justice located around different images and techniques, their message generally captured by Auerbach's (1983) allusion to *Justice Without Law*. Initiatives around the various mantles of informal justice, neighbourhood justice, alternative dispute resolution and community justice have contested law's implicit mandate to secure justice. Most recently, an amorphous grouping of initiatives under the rubric of restorative justice has come into its own, especially in youth justice arenas.

During that time, much figurative ink has flowed in attempts to describe and define restorative justice.[1] Even if its proponents do not always agree on the implications of the justice they

---

1 The discourse often alludes to 'alternative dispute resolution' (ADR), 'informal', 'community' or 'restorative justice'. Though not always interchangeable, these terms tend to correspond to evolving identities; throughout the 1990s, however, restorative justice became an encompassing – and perhaps dominant – sign that included reference to various informal and community options (McLaughlin *et al*, 2003; Roche, 2003). ADR tends still to be used in legal circles. One could also note attempts to distinguish restorative and community justice (Crawford and Clear, 2003; Clear and Karp, 2002). Without spurning these debates, the present analysis focuses on restorative justice as a broad identity established in proponents' discourses, with inevitable genealogical references to ADR, informalism and community justice.

pursue, most define its auspices in common ways. It is depicted as a different approach to crime from what is on offer in criminal justice domains. For them, restorative justice works from a distinctive moral compass, pointing to a justice that requires the active input of victims, offenders and affected community members to heal the harm of a specific criminal act. One of its leading proponents defines the terrain thus:

> Restorative justice is a process to involve, to the extent possible, those who have a stake in a specific offense and to collectively identify and address harms, needs, and obligations, in order to heal and to put things as right as possible (Zehr, 2002: 37).

Elaborating further, Umbreit notes:

> Restorative justice is a victim-centered response to crime that gives the individuals most directly affected by the criminal act – the victim, the offender, their families, and representatives from the community – the opportunity to be directly involved in responding to the harm caused by crime (Umbreit, 2001: xxxvii).

From this vantage point, restorative justice is contrasted with courtroom justice and the moral frameworks associated with adversarial retribution. Restorative justice visions explicitly reject principles of justice that derive from *lex talionis*, or the desire to punish guilty offenders on the basis of 'an eye for an eye … '. The purpose of restorative justice is not to isolate the guilty so that the state can exact its 'pound of flesh'. Instead, its version of justice is centred on specifically nuanced concepts of harm, obligation, need, restoration, healing, reconciliation, reintegration, participation and – when appropriate – forgiveness.

These values are then used to guide community-based, victim-centred approaches to crime, requiring offenders to make amends for their criminal behaviours (eg, Zehr, 2002; Strang, 2001). Restorative justice offers a practical, problem-solving approach that deals with 'real' people rather than abstract legal rules – an expansive range of processes, programs and practices designed to empower victims, offenders and communities to redress the material, psychological and relational harms generated by crime. Such forums promote active 'dialogue and participatory decision-making' while encouraging offenders to take responsibility for their actions (Zehr, 2002: 55). The most commonly deployed restorative justice practices include family group conferences, community mediation and panels, victim-offender mediations, sentencing circles, reconciliation commissions, and various informal tribunals (see Roche, 2003: 6; McLaughlin *et al*, 2003).

Family group conferences are among the most emblematic forms of restorative justice. Despite differences in programs, family group conferences are most prominent in the youth justice field and usually entail structured meetings between victims, offenders and other community support people. In general, they follow the commission of offences where an offender (often a youth) is accused of, and admits to committing, a crime as defined in legal statute.[2] The offender agrees (after being referred usually by the police, judges, community agency workers, etc) to participate in a family group conference in place of dealing with the matter through criminal justice processes. Co-ordinators, who are often employed within community policing or justice departments, arrange the conferences by contacting victims and outlining some of the benefits of attending such meetings. They are encouraged to attend with family, friends and other community support people, and to consider how offenders might make things right for them. The conferences are often held at community venues and chaired by 'referees' who introduce offenders, victims and their respective families/support people. Referees may be community volunteers, agency workers, community police officers, youth justice workers, and so on (Johnstone, 2003). They employ diverse mediation techniques to facilitate discussions that require offenders to confront the harm they have caused to victims and take responsibility for the offence. At the same time, victims and families are given an opportunity to make their views, needs and wants clear – all are involved in discussions of how offenders might make meaningful amends in context. The aim is to restore 'right relations' in the community by involving all participants, but ensuring that the victim's needs are at the forefront of conference discussions.

Kurki (2003), Clear and Karp (2002) and Morris (1995, 2000) describe various 'community mediation' processes where community volunteers are involved in assisting affected subjects to develop appropriate responses to conflict and crime. These broadly formulated community processes include: mediation sessions in which local mediators (volunteer or paid) assist participants to define key issues arising out of a given event and develop ways of redressing community relations disturbed by criminal events; community panels or boards consisting of

---

2 See Bazemore and Umbreit (2003) for an analysis of four different conferencing models. See also Bazemore and Umbreit (1995).

volunteer community members that 'hear' disputes and help disputants to resolve conflict (Merry and Milner, 1993; Karp and Walther, 2001); and the use of respected community elders as conciliators at the behest of participants to a given conflict. In addition, Umbreit (2001) provides a detailed analysis of victim-offender mediation that applies mediation techniques designed specifically to heal relationships between victims, offenders and community stakeholders. In many cases, as the name implies, this mediation occurs once offenders are convicted by courts; it is not a diversionary process as such. There are also various restorative processes that claim the rubric of sentencing circles, specifically designed to involve affected community members to help arrive at contextually appropriate sentences for offenders (see Canada, 2003; Stuart, 2001).

Although diverse, these various images and techniques are considered more or less restorative depending on the extent to which they embrace a loosely defined set of restorative values and principles (Zehr, 2002: 55). Restorative justice's defining moral values are thus elemental to the programs deployed in its name, yet these values are able to achieve prominence in rather specific socio-political and cultural contexts, and betray a complex genealogical lineage. Although this is not the place to detail the complex rise of restorative justice, it is nevertheless instructive to sketch elements of its lineage. If nothing else, this should serve to point out broader lines of descent that have contributed to the emergence of values and practices associated with the identity of restorative justice.

An abbreviated genealogy of restorative justice

Amidst perceptions of growing poverty and dissent in the 1950s and 1960s, numerous international governmental initiatives focused attention on social defence, community development and various poverty reduction strategies.[3] In addition, social defence strategies arose in the wake of the Second World War, effectively employing military reasoning to defend 'society' against anti-social threats, especially from a so-called 'criminal

---

3 For example, in the United States the Mobilization for Youth program offered a widespread sociological attempt to break cycles of poverty by improving community facilities, housing, health, education, and so on in impoverished areas.

element'. With the active encouragement of the United Nations, an emphasis on preventing crime helped to establish criminology departments in many academic institutions (Walters, 2003). The aim was to develop strategic knowledge designed to reduce crime, deviance and conflicts that threatened normal social relations.

In a related fashion, and in response to rioting in inner city ghettos, the United States government developed 'upliftment' strategies that established a Community Relations Service during the same period. Charged with the task of developing communities, this service provided important resources for the advance of neighbourhood justice (Hofrichter, 1987), ADR, community mediation (see Pavlich, 1996a), community panels (Merry and Milner, 1993) and community justice (Shonholtz, 1988/89). From the early 1980s, these developments fed into, and elaborated upon, a growing sense that local community strength is foundational to vibrant social democracies (Shonholtz, 1988/89). Later, advocates would develop this sense into a call for strong community-based civil societies as the basis for democracy (Strang and Braithwaite, 2001).

The rebirth of communitarian discourses provided another cultural resource for those championing community forms of justice (Clear and Karp, 2002; Etzioni, 1998). Coterminous with attempts to build security through communities, one finds in the 1970s and 1980s increasingly regular critiques, especially by state-sanctioned law reform bodies, of the adversarial legal system. The criminal justice system was seen to be failing, and to be doing so with spectacularly tragic consequences for the social fabric. The law was depicted as deploying anachronistic institutions ill-equipped to accommodate the changing volume, type and causes of dispute in the late 20th century.[4] The system was labelled as costly, inefficient, alienating, arbitrary, inaccessible, and inappropriately focused on the interests of lawyers and judges. Punishment regimes were, at the same time, a realm of dystopian criminological thinking: this was the era of the so-called 'nothing works' thesis – neither punishing offenders nor attempting to rehabilitate them seemed to curtail recidivism. All of this helped the informalism cause and its promise to offer

---

4 See, for example, Ford Foundation (1978), Fisher (1975) and Frank (1970).

another way to deal with crime. Law reformers saw in informal justice a method to resolve disputes in more lasting ways.

Within this informal justice ethos, legal anthropology struck a reverberating chord with its descriptions of Barotse jurisprudence (Gluckman, 1965), justice amongst the Tiv (Bohannan, 1957), or the fascinating ways in which moots/tribunals sought justice in various African contexts (Fisher, 1975). A developing 'access to justice' movement appealed to these analyses in its attempts to make Western legality more accessible to people and communities (Auerbach, 1983).[5] In addition, the rise of an alternative dispute resolution movement, the call for greater informality in 'minor cases' (Frank, 1970) and the funding of experiments in neighbourhood justice in the United States (Ford Foundation, 1978) rendered the search for justice outside law practicable. Allied to such experiments, various churches (especially the Mennonite Central Committee) deployed community justice initiatives in the United States, Canada, Britain and New Zealand.[6] To be sure, the now-pervasive values of restoration, healing, reintegration, forgiveness and compassion within restorative governmentalities often derive from theological roots. Church-based restorative justice initiatives seemed to align particularly well with community mediation/panels and victim-offender reconciliation programs (more recently renamed victim-offender mediation – see Umbreit, 2001).

In sum, restorative justice's lineage includes the single and combined effects of: poverty reduction, community development and social defence initiatives; a rising informal justice movement bolstered by findings from legal anthropology coupled with a resonant critique of Western legal forms; and high profile experiments with informal justice, including those relying on theological images and concepts. This lineage should be silhouetted against rising neo-liberal backgrounds with their various, but concentrated, attacks on social welfare state formations. They are also very much part of the social landscapes that have brought many Western contexts into what Garland identifies as vast cultures of crime control (see Garland, 2001). Calls for non-state justice thrived amidst a great chorus booming

---

5 See generally Abel (1982).
6 For example, Zehr (1990), Van Ness and Strong (2002), Umbreit (2001), Peachey (2003), Consedine (1995), Morris and Young (1987) and Marshall (2003).

the necessity of private, free markets to regulate individual subjects outside state institutions or public bodies. Such corporatising attacks on the social welfare state were often successful in fragmenting general images of welfare society into private communities (the social appearing more as a 'community of communities'– see Etzioni, 1998). They also supported the concept of diverting (especially young) offenders from state courts into communities for first (and other) offences, and enabled advocates of restorative justice to champion the cause of individual participation in communal approaches to criminal events.

Of course, this genealogical lineage is both sketchy and incomplete, but it does at least allude to patterns of descent that comprise the context within which restorative justice's shifting identity emerges. But how is one to decipher theoretically the emergence of restorative justice? Over the years, the rise of restorative justice has been debated through numerous theoretical analyses and assessments.[7]

The early contours of these debates centred on the question of whether informal justice (and ADR) did, as its proponents allege, actually wrest control over disputes away from the seemingly omniscient and alienating social welfare state (Pavlich, 1996b). Advocates argued that informal justice created everyday domains of freedom that empowered communities and individual disputants to resolve disputes without relying on state justice (hence ADR). Victim-offender mediation (reconciliation) programs extended the idea of mediation by seeking to reconcile parties involved in criminal events, opening the way to broader restorative attempts to deal with the harms of crime. Supporters saw informal measures as creating new pathways to justice that empowered individual victims, offenders, disputants and communities to wrest back control of conflict from state institutions (Christie, 1977). In this way, informal justice was seen to diminish state control and to broaden the scope for community participation (Shonholtz, 1988/89).

Neo-Marxist critics of such justice, by contrast, pointed to pernicious ways in which community mediation expanded state control by other means. Any retraction of state control was mere

---

7 See, eg, Abel (1982), Harrington (1985), Hofrichter (1987), Matthews (1988), Roche (2003), Pavlich (1996a, 1996b) and Johnstone (2003).

rhetoric, since informal justice mechanisms were doing the state's job.[8] The ideology of receding state control effectively masked the reality that informalism enabled the state to extend and intensify its control over individual lives. The welfare state could thereby deal with protracted legitimacy and fiscal crises of the 1970s by turning over 'minor' cases to volunteers in the community; however, in practice, it remained firmly in control of the finances, authorisation and even case loads for given programs. This, for the critics, indicated the extent to which the state was widening and intensifying its control network while claiming to do precisely the opposite.

In response to this debate, some argued that the entire focus on state expansion or retraction – the net widening argument – was somewhat misconceived for several reasons.[9] Key amongst these was the thorny issue of how to define the state precisely enough to judge any declarations of expanded or retracted control. Drawing on Foucault's work, some thus proposed conceptualising community mediation as embodying a new constellation of power-knowledge relations deployed in the name of justice. By exploring the models of power introduced by community justice, one could then chart its alignments with, or separations from, law-sovereign and disciplinary political models. The aim was to describe the nuances, and assess the dangers/yields, of the emerging power arrangements (Pavlich, 1996a). Through such discussions, Foucault's concept of 'governmentality' seemed to provide a potentially valuable theoretical grid with which to conceptualise restorative justice. It is to this concept that I now turn.

Governmentality, rationale and technique

We have alluded to broad contours of restorative justice, but what sort of political logic, governmental rationale, attends to its adherents' activities? How do they understand what it is that they are attempting to do? Raising such questions alerts us to the 'mentalities' through which people seek to govern, rendering Foucault's notion of 'governmentality' directly pertinent. Although many have now contributed to discussions of 'governmentality', I interpret Foucault rather specifically as

---

8 For instance, see Abel (1982) and Hofrichter (1987).

9 See Pavlich (1996a, 1996b) for a discussion of this point.

deliberately mobilising the concept in three related ways.[10] First, he uses the term 'governmentality' to extend his analysis of how early modern power relations developed alongside the dominant medieval 'law-sovereign' models of power. Here, governmentality names configurations of power relations, dating from around the 16th century, related to practices of cameralism and police science, but now re-directed to specifying (and thus controlling) the nature of subjects in populations. Though allied with disciplinary and law-sovereign power relations, governmentality was uniquely concerned with shaping human 'nature', life, and not correcting (normalising) or judging (punishing) individuals. It is deployed coterminously, and in complex contextual amalgams, with the other forms of power. In many ways, derivations of this form of governance are locatable in various neo-liberal auspices that frame the rise of restorative justice (Pavlich, 2000).

Secondly, one might refer to Bentham (1890) to get a sense of the less than visible ways in which governmentality operates. He distinguishes between two sorts of control: on the one hand there is direct, visible state coercion targeting undesired action and used *inter alia* for its immediate as well as deterrent effects; on the other, there is a less visible 'indirect' way of governing, less concerned with action than with shaping the 'will' and 'motivations' that produce particular actions (for example, he notes the potential role of secret agents and spies in securing such effects). The latter gives a sense of how governmentality is concerned with what Foucault calls the 'conduct of conduct', subtly arranging background settings to produce subjects who think and act in ways that do not require direct coercion. Self-governing subjects are produced when the latter buy into the logic and formulated identities of a given governmentality. This is why liberal rule can be seen to 'govern through freedom' to the extent that the freedoms presumed to inhere in particular subjects are already manipulated by framing techniques (Rose, 1999). It also suggests how many of the values championed by proponents of restorative justice (eg, healing, restoration, individual empowerment, etc), and the techniques used (eg, mediation, conferencing) could be seen as indirect attempts to shape the motivations (and actions) of subjects somehow

---

10 For references to the larger debates on this, see Dean (1999) and Rose (1999).

involved in criminal events. Additionally, on another level, viewing restorative justice as a governmentality makes theoretical sense of the manner in which restorative approaches distinguish themselves from the punitive coercions of criminal justice.

Thirdly, the term suggests how power both creates and is created by the subjects entangled within its orbits. One might point to the 'mentalities' that establish apparatuses of understanding, meaning horizons, to enable particular methods of ruling. These mentalities of governance entail specific political rationalities; as logics of how to rule, they define such matters as what is governed, who is governed, who does the governing and what governing itself properly entails. Such govern*mentalities* render particular ideas and practices (rationales and techniques of governing) understandable, conceivable, viable and indeed practicable. The rationales for, say, family group and victim-offender conferences make sense of how restorative techniques are to be deployed, as well as to whom they should be addressed, etc. Both rationales and techniques comprise 'governmentalities' in the sense that I shall evoke the concept.

Although I do refer to all three aspects of the concept 'governmentality' throughout this book, it is the last which is employed in a sustained and deliberate fashion. Specifically, I focus on the 'mentalities' of governance that supporters use to make sense of the practices claiming the name 'restorative justice'. These 'restorative governmentalities', as I shall call them, not only help us to deploy practices of restorative governance (eg, family group conferences, victim-offender mediation, etc), but render them meaningful, rational, practicable and understandable to those concerned.[11] They deploy mentalities that help subjects to define what it is that they are doing when they govern through images of restorative justice, and thereby demarcate appropriate ways of so governing. I focus especially on advocates' mentalities – the influential rationales and ideas

---

11 In using the term in this way, I have alluded to the problem of whether to use the singular 'governmentality' or plural 'governmentalities'. For the most part, I have opted for the plural form to keep firmly in mind that even if there are common tendencies, there are diverse restorative justice 'mentalities' (say, those addressing victims, or offenders, etc) that combine in complex ways within the broad political terrain that restorative justice has come to occupy. In relatively fewer places, the singular 'governmentality' is used to connote a specific instance of broader restorative justice governmentalities.

contained in their discourse directed to what restorative justice practice entails. My concern is with the underlying 'grids of understanding', the meaning horizons, that formulate logics and rationales for calculating and instituting justice in one way rather than another.

Restorative governmentalities

What regulatory techniques do restorative justice rationales of governance licence as 'alternatives' to criminal justice? It is perhaps useful at this point briefly to indicate how restorative governmentalities frame: (1) the object of governance (harm); (2) visions of who is governed; (3) the designated governors; and (4) indications of what appropriate governance entails.

What is governed? Restorative justice carves out a specific conception of the appropriate object for its governance – as distinct from criminal justice agencies. As noted, the criticisms restorative justice advocates level against state justice are precisely that its institutions focus on determining guilt and emphasise ways of coercing (punishing) the offender. To the extent that it uses adversarial methods to determine whether a violation of abstract criminal law has occurred, this system governs 'crime' (or perhaps, through notions of 'crime'). By contrast, restorative governmentalities approach justice through a value framework directed to the *harms* caused by crime (Strang and Braithwaite, 2001: 1–2). 'Simply put,' as McCold and Wachtel note, 'restorative justice is the process involving the direct stakeholders in determining how best to repair the harm done by offending behaviour' (2002: 111). One detects here a rationale which posits repairing or healing harm as a guiding moral vector.

Who is governed? Restorative governmentalities distinguish themselves from criminal justice agencies by directing their regulatory techniques to a broadly defined group of stakeholders, beyond a focus on the 'offender' (Braithwaite, 2002: 16–26). The claim resonates throughout the governmentality. Umbreit notes that the main targets of restorative governance are 'victims, offenders, their families, and representatives from the community' (2001: xxxvii). McCold and Wachtel take as 'obvious' that 'One should always try to involve victims, offenders and their communities of care in responses to crime' (2002: 139).

In short, rather than focusing on the guilt of those accused of a crime, devising appropriate punishments or applying abstracted legal categories, restorative justice proponents target the lives of offenders, victims and those affected by a criminal event in a given community. Such stakeholder identities are meant to be fluid and transient. For example, victims are encouraged to embrace an alternative identity once they have resolved some of the issues surrounding a criminal offence (see Sharpe, 1998). Similarly, offenders – once they have 'repaired' the harms caused by their actions, and perhaps been 'reintegratively shamed' – are inveighed to shed the offender identity (Braithwaite, 1989). In addition, communities of interest that form around a given criminal event are unlikely to persist as agents of justice once matters have been resolved.

Such formulations of who is governed serve as a way to differentiate restorative justice from criminal justice system practices that focus on abstract notions of legal persons and/or offenders. On top of this, once an individual is identified as a criminal offender, the label tends to be remarkably enduring, with enormous consequences. Restorative justice targets, by contrast, real people (not abstract legal entities) through governmental processes that focus on harms that crime generates for victims, communities and individual offenders. One might also note the emphasis placed on positioning restorative justice as a victim-centred approach, and the related attempt to cast this as a better alternative to the criminal justice system's focus on establishing the guilt or innocence of offenders.

Who governs? Another alleged point of difference between restorative and criminal justice concerns the agents of control – the governors. Restorative discourses are relatively clear in their criticism of the criminal justice system for usurping historical power from victims and local communities and consolidating authority in centralised institutions (Braithwaite, 2002; see also Johnstone, 2002). Because the governors of state agencies include such agents as the police, lawyers, judges, correctional officers, probation officers, etc, the state's control is exerted by impartial, impersonal officials who may not have a direct understanding (or share the interests) of those affected by a given criminal offence. Those with an active interest in a given event are typically removed from a case because of a perceived conflict of interest. The quest for an equal and fair rule of law demands a degree of impersonality from its agents.

In contrast to such governors, restorative governmentalities aim to empower community agents directly affected by a given conflict. Their emotional, interest-driven and value-based relation to the events is esteemed as essential to defining local instances of criminal harm. Such agents vary from family group conference co-ordinators, referees, family members, friends and church-based volunteers, to mediators and community panel organisers. An emphasised point of dissimilarity between the governors of the two approaches to justice is the deliberately personal and involved nature of restorative agents as opposed to the relatively impersonal, even bureaucratised, governors of criminal justice.

What is appropriate governing? We have already indicated how restorative governmentalities describe themselves as quite different from state forms by virtue of their explicit allegiance to restorative values (Johnstone, 2003; Braithwaite, 2002; Umbreit, 2001). The latter seek future-directed, pragmatic, problem-solving processes designed to repair, restore and effectively redress the harms of crime. In this regard, restorative justice governance could be described as a 'method of bringing together all stake-holders in an undominated dialogue about the consequences of injustice and what is to be done to put them right' (Braithwaite, 2002: 12). As opposed to the criminal justice system that reactively focuses its adversarial methods on past events to determine guilt, restorative processes govern by helping stakeholders to define, and develop ways to heal, the harms of crime. As such, restorative justice is seen to be a 'modest philosophy' that:

> ... settles for the procedural requirement that parties talk until they feel that harmony has been restored on the basis of a discussion of all the injustices they see as relevant to the case (Braithwaite, 2002: 87).

The problem-solving governmental techniques are directed to governing the future.

Therefore, restorative governmentalities seek to distinguish themselves from criminal justice agencies by claiming unique objects, subjects, agents and processes to deal with criminal events.[12] However, a closer look at the attempt to sustain this governmentality as a viable *alternative* to the criminal justice model reveals a paradox: while positing itself as a distinct

---

12 One interpretation of this point dovetails with the overall orientation in which governmentality is different from, but related to, both law-sovereign and disciplinary models of power.

alternative, restorative justice also predicates itself on key concepts within the criminal justice system. As an alternative, it is presented as a separate and autonomous entity; yet its foundational concepts derive from the very system it claims to substitute. This paradox is worth exploring, since it pervades vast areas of restorative governmentalities; its contours remain silently embedded in the very auspices of their programs. Focusing explicitly on the paradox is instructive and provides a method of grappling with the difficulties inherent in seeking to provide alternative calculations of justice.

The *imitor* paradox and restorative justice

imitor: to imitate, substitute

paradox: para – opposite of, contrary; doxa – opinion

Etymologically, the term *paradox* derives from the Latin *paradoxum* and the Greek *paradoxon*. The prefix *para-* denotes 'opposite of', 'contrary to' or 'altered'; the noun stem *doxa* refers to received 'opinion' (Ayto, 1990). When conjoined, these parts have over centuries come to denote a sense of surprise, something 'contrary to expectation'. In the context of this book, I mean that there is an unexpected mystery, an intractable bifurcation that *simultaneously* occasions two logically conflicting strands of thought at the very heart of restorative governmentalities. The Latin *imitor* connotes both substitution and imitation; perhaps one could even make it work as an aporetic formulation of 'substitution through imitation'. In any case, in this book *imitor* is used to evoke how restorative justice modalities that claim to be substitutes for something else often end up imitating the very thing from which distance is sought. The ensuing *imitor* paradox entails an unexpected tension that allows restorative justice to exist as a seemingly singular, internally consistent entity even though it is simultaneously committed to two opposing foundations: namely, as substitute for and imitator of criminal justice concepts and institutions. In short, restorative justice defines its governmentalities in opposition to basic concepts within the criminal justice system, but it does so by founding itself on many of those self-same concepts (eg, crime, victim, offender and community).

Throughout what follows, then, the paradox of *imitor* is used to connote restorative governmentalities' simultaneous attempt to offer a substitute for criminal justice whilst predicating themselves on (and so imitating) existing criminal justice arrangements. The Latin *imitor* provides no more than a useful shortcut to remind us of the substitution and imitation comprising the paradox of a supposedly independent restorative justice that ensnares itself within criminal justice language, logic and agencies.

Before outlining the broad contours of restorative justice's *imitor* paradox, it is important to offer two significant caveats. First, alluding to the idea of paradox is not meant to annul restorative justice's achievements, or to nullify its claims. Arguing that the shape of an entity like restorative justice is made possible because of a founding paradox does not cancel its tangible effects on everyday life. Rather, one might say that the presence of any identity is enabled as much by aporetic absences as by anything else (Derrida, 1976, 1995). Presence and order are predicated on absence, rupture and disorder. This is especially apparent in attempts to project images of justice outside of a given ethos, but doing so by relying on the available language of that ethos – fashioning justice anew is always to some extent bound to use the significations of old. Bringing this paradox to the fore is meant to open the analysis up to the complexities and seductions involved when attempting to calculate justice in excess of dominant criminal justice images.

Secondly, it is important to note that this book taps into common terms and concepts within restorative justice governmentalities, but my own formulations do not necessarily align with the former. For example, the ease with which restorative justice advocates contrast their justice with that of 'criminal justice' may well involve a reification that occludes the complex plurality of ideas, practices and institutions claiming this rubric. Since the following analysis focuses on, and taps into, influential strands of restorative justice discourse, however problematic the notions may appear, its purpose is not so much to evaluate concepts *per se* as it is to explore the contours and consequences of a paradox associated with that governmentality.

With these caveats in mind, let us now turn to the two broad elements of restorative justice's *imitor* paradox. This discussion serves as a prelude to this book's more detailed inspection of specific ways in which the paradox is reproduced through restorative governmentalities' versions of values and processes.

Restorative justice: an independent alternative to criminal justice

Advocates of restorative justice posit their values and practices as independent of the coercive approach of the criminal justice system. The claim that restorative processes provide an idiosyncratic vision of, as well as approach to, justice is made in various ways within the proponents' discourses. All, however, start with versions of the following basic critique: 'no one is satisfied with our criminal justice system' (Sharpe, 1998: 2). Victims, lawyers, prosecutors, judges, the accused and the community are said to be confused, alienated, hurt or frustrated by the existing system. Hence:

> It seems clear that there must be a better way to do things ... it won't be enough to run the present system more efficiently. Instead of doing more, it is time to do something *different*. A good place to start is with a broad understanding of what crime does, and a different understanding of what justice demands (Sharpe, 1998: 2).

The call for a 'different understanding of what justice demands' presents restorative justice as quite different from, even incommensurable with, the moral principles guiding criminal justice. Thus, Braithwaite underscores the importance of 'the idea of restorative justice as an alternative that has a very different value framing than punitive justice' (2002: 12). For him and many other advocates, restorative justice pursues values directed at healing as opposed to determining guilt, innocence, punishment and retribution (Johnstone, 2002; Graef, 2001). The understanding isolates a different moral 'lens' for approaching justice. Zehr's (2002, 1990) seminal formulation, for example, proffers an alternative 'paradigm of justice': the state's retributive approach to justice is set against restorative justice's victim-centred, restitutive, repentance-based approach. Umbreit (2001: xxviii–xxix) too offers moral principles (values) that reflect restorative justice's 'truly different paradigm'. These include an emphasis on the restoration of victims and victimised communities, victim participation, offender responsibility rather than punishment, community involvement, and responsibility for 'social conditions that contribute to offender behaviour' (2001: xxix).

In such formulations, its supporters evoke restorative justice as a distinguishable entity through a now familiar rhetoric of contrasts. The strident critiques of the values as well as the processes of criminal justice systems provide a starting point for enunciating restorative governmentalities as a distinct ontology. Its opposition to adversarial, retributive, courtroom values and procedures thus defines restorative justice. Stated differently, the very coherence of this alternative governmentality rests on the presupposition of difference: restorative justice announces itself as ethically, ontologically and practically distinct from the rationales, images and practices of state criminal justice.

Defining itself as an alternative through its challenges to the failures of the state's criminal justice system, restorative justice asserts a distinct identity, capable of relatively autochthonous development. On this basis, we can understand the advocates' call to develop uniquely restorative – as opposed to criminal – justice practices. And the quest for an alternative form of justice is no tangent: it is inextricably bound to restorative justice's ability to enunciate itself as a distinctive identity. Braithwaite makes the point succinctly:

> If we take restorative justice seriously, it involves a very different way of thinking about traditional notions such as deterrence, rehabilitation, incapacitation, and crime prevention. It also means transformed foundations of criminal jurisprudence and of our notions of freedom, democracy, and community (2002: 4–5).

Referring to such profound differences allows proponents to justify restorative justice as a viable way of governing crime-affected subjects in its own right and on its own terms. As a 'different way of thinking' that transforms the 'foundations of criminal jurisprudence', restorative justice emerges as a distinctly new method of approaching both crime and justice. It is said to emanate from community-based traditions predating criminal justice, and operate from an entirely different moral compass (Zehr, 1990). Its emphasis on values of compassionate, humane, forgiving, community-orientated, voluntary, victim-centred justice is diametrically opposed to adversarial retribution; it also licences particular practices like family group conferences, community panels and mediation.[13] Consequently, in this area of the discourse, proponents distinguish restorative justice by defining its rationales and practices as *fundamentally* incommensurable with, and independent of, state criminal justice agencies.

---

13 See generally Johnstone (2003), but also Walgrave (2002b), Braithwaite (2002), Umbreit (2001) and Zehr (1990, 1995).

Restorative justice: appendage to criminal justice

Restorative justice's self-assessment as fundamentally incommensurable with state criminal justice rationales is found alongside an equally influential contention that pulls restorative governmentalities in an entirely opposite direction. Here, proponents propose that restorative justice be seen as working within, and as a basic complement to the demands of, state criminal justice. Bazemore and McLeod (2002), Cooley (1999), and even Zehr (2002) dilute the concept of 'alternative' by giving it much more of a local, parochial meaning where restorative justice is seen as providing limited alternatives to aspects of the existing criminal justice system. So, restorative justice may be seen as offering an alternative to 'courtroom procedures' or 'penalty regimes' within the criminal justice system, but not to the criminal justice system itself. That is, restorative justice is not here positioned as an alternative to the criminal justice rationales and practices but as an *alternative to specific processes provided within that system*. In this mode, restorative justice emerges as an appendage to enhance (perhaps even expand) existing criminal justice and/or legal institutions. Where, for example, the state's youth justice system emphasises family values and the role of the community, restorative justice steps up to the plate by delivering family group conferences as appended alternatives to youth courts.

Here, the bold claims surrounding restorative justice's independent identity as a new form of justice dissolve into enunciations as a subordinated component, reform, to be housed *within* criminal justice institutions. The discourse now commits restorative justice *in advance* to complementing bits of a predefined regulatory field. Cooley adroitly summarises this point in the following terms:

> Restorative justice approaches turn on the existence of a wrong. Restorative justice begins with the premise that a wrong has occurred. *Restorative justice works well within the criminal justice system because the criminal law provides a ready-made list of wrongs and an easily identifiable wrongdoer* ... For restorative justice, because the culpability of the wrongdoer is taken for granted, determining what happened is important only to redress the wrong (1999: 3; emphasis added).

Bazemore and McLeod echo the 'working well within the criminal justice system' idea by enunciating the following goal of restorative justice: ' ... to demonstrate real change in the nature of social control so that government assumes a supportive role in facilitating informal community-driven processes' (2002: 167–68). They continue:

> ... informalism alone, especially the romantic kind that some restorative justice advocates seem to promote, is insufficient ... Therefore, restorative justice implementation must be tied to an equal emphasis on a strong social welfare state ... (2002: 168).

Consequently, it is not surprising that, in practice, as Johnstone's (2002: 163–65)[14] synopsis of the field shows, restorative justice programs tend to work within (rather than against) state criminal justice arenas.[15]

As a result, restorative justice programs have been lauded as exemplary success stories, especially those deployed under the auspices of state justice institutions. For instance, restorative programs at Wagga Wagga, Australia (Moore and O'Connell, 2003), New Zealand (Maxwell and Morris, 1993), Thames Valley (Pollard, 2001; see also Umbreit, 2001: Chapter 12) and various victim-offender mediation programs in the United States (see Umbreit, 2001: Chapter 10) all operate as self-enunciated complements to existing criminal justice systems. As appended complements, they are usually evaluated, vetted, approved, funded (wholly or mainly) and even initiated by state officials. Many too rely on state agencies for their case loads and their institutional survival depends on the active support of various state agencies (community police, probation departments, justice departments, crime prevention units, etc). For a declared alternative, one might observe, restorative justice is doing rather well within existing systems.

The overwhelming practical consequence of restorative justice operating as an appended complement to juridical terrains is the development of programs that serve criminal justice institutions.

---

14 In particular, Johnstone argues that restorative justice works as part of state control apparatuses in various ways, and tends to operate by: providing a 'modified civil procedure' for dealing with crime in different ways; developing a 'parallel track' for dealing with crime locally in communities; or forming part of the state's responses to crime (as 'parallel but interrelated tracks').

15 Programs accordingly may work within state justice arenas to secure better attachments to republican ideals (Braithwaite, 2002; Shonholtz, 1988/89), civil society (Strang and Braithwaite, 2001; Peachey, 2003), communitarian values (Morris, 2000; Dignan and Cavadino, 1996), victim rights, offender responsibilisation, etc.

Clearly, the aim here is not to challenge state-based criminal justice arrangements, as might be expected from an independent alternative deemed to be the very opposite of retributive justice. Rather, restorative justice is then espoused as a way of enhancing state agencies, and ironically furthering or elaborating upon state criminal justice arenas.

The imitor paradox

> The basic problem is of course whether we consider restorative justice as merely a series of techniques which are to be integrated into the existing systems of penal or re-educative responses to crime or restorative justice has to become a fully fledged alternative which should in the longer term replace maximally the existing systems (Walgrave, 1998: 12).

Walgrave's insightful formulation of the situation traces the *imitor* paradox precisely.[16] There are two bifurcated strands of thought associated with restorative justice that amount to a paradox at the heart of its governmentality. On the one hand, restorative justice is presented as a distinct form of justice that exists *sui generis*, making sense of advocates' claims that they are offering/deploying a form of justice which is ethically and practically distinct from criminal justice institutions.[17] On the other hand, the restorative paradigm claims relevance and success by presenting itself as a component of reform within existing criminal justice systems. The former suggests an image of justice decidedly *contra* to criminal incarnations and having a coherence in its own right. The overall effect is to generate an irresolvable, aporetic structure that simultaneously sees itself as independent of, yet is constitutively dependent upon, criminal

---

16 The point is echoed in Johnstone's assessment that:

> One of the central tensions within the restorative justice movement is over its relationship to the conventional criminal justice system … Proponents of restorative justice frequently espouse the ambitious goal of creating a radical alternative to state criminal justice: a new paradigm of justice which will be community-based, treat offenders with respect and meet the needs of victims. In practice, however, many are developing restorative justice as a set of programs within criminal justice systems that are predominantly shaped by and reflect more conventional (non restorative) concepts, assumptions and commitments (2003: 359).

17 See Walgrave (2000, 2002a) for some insight into the 'maximalist' debates that relate to this point.

justice.[18] Restorative governmentalities' commitment to both sides of this tension produces a paradoxical foundation that has important consequences for the current identity of what we take to be restorative justice in particular, and more broadly for the possibility of conceptualising alternative visions of justice.

This *imitor* paradox could be considered a *leitmotif* that recurs throughout restorative governmentalities. In the chapters of this book, I analyse different dimensions of the paradox. In particular, I chart how it is replicated in ethical domains that articulate the 'values' of restorative governmentalities (Chapter 2) as well as in discussions of governmental 'processes' directed towards victims (Chapter 3), offenders (Chapter 4) and communities (Chapter 5).[19] Both values and practices embrace complex political rationalities, but I will focus on how, in each context, the aspiration to promote a distinct moral and practical alternative to criminal justice is undermined by the manner in which restorative justice positions itself as supplementary and ultimately subordinate to state justice empires.

Aporetic restorative values

Specifically, Chapter 2 focuses its attention on the moral frameworks enunciated by restorative governmentalities as a means of distinguishing a uniquely restorative variety of justice. These frameworks play an important role in restorative governmentalities because, as Sharpe indicates, 'Restorative justice does not have a prescribed protocol' (1998: 19). Instead, specific programs find ways of incorporating restorative values and principles when 'doing justice' in restorative ways (see Zehr,

---

18 Some proponents try to elide the tension by positing restorative and criminal justice as the extremes of a broad justice continuum, seeking to move current institutions in more of a restorative direction (Zehr, 2002: 58). Also, Braithwaite calls for a 'responsive regulation' approach that progressively moves from restorative justice, to deterrence and then to incapacitation (2002: 29–42). However, these do not escape the paradox because the very different conceptions of justice remain fully intact. The problem then becomes this: how can it be feasible to collapse vastly different traditions, values, processes, paradigms and approaches (restorative versus retributive) into a single, commensurable continuum? If the paradigms are so different, as claimed, then it is difficult to see how they can be so reduced as to render them common or continuous. The logic of providing alternatives stands uneasily against the very idea of continuums.

19 Strang and Braithwaite (2001: 1) appositely isolate values and processes as prominent areas to which advocates have dedicated much attention.

2002). We have already alluded to the claimed moral difference between restorative and criminal justice. Within the governmentality, this difference hinges on a distinction between a restorative healing of harms generated by crime (with an emphasis on healing, compassion, restitution, victim-centredness, forgiveness, restoring right relations in communities, etc) versus a retributive punishment of criminal offenders (with its emphasis on adversarial guilt-seeking, punitive pay-back, deterrence, offenders, etc).

Such distinctions are not quite as clear-cut as they sound, because the restorative value of healing harm is predicated upon criminal justice systems' definitions of crime (see Daly, 2003b); crime is the foundation, and restorative justice deals with its 'aftermath' in unique ways. In other words, the purportedly different moral framework derives directly from the very justice it is said to challenge. The paradox is replicated at the level of formulating moral guidelines that supposedly designate a radically different vision of justice.

Paradox, technique and process

If the *imitor* paradox shadows the values of restorative governmentalities, it also traces the mentalities associated with techniques for governing victims, offenders and communities. Chapter 3 examines how restorative justice articulates itself as different from criminal justice by emphasising forms of victim empowerment alien to the courtroom. Against what it describes as retribution's offender focus, restorative justice claims to deploy victim-centred processes that encourage the active participation of those harmed by crime. At the same time, however, the governmentality clings to notions that victims are borne in the aftermath of crime, thereby presuming the existence of both 'victims' and 'crime' as defined by legal jurisprudence. This tendency to assume and simultaneously transcend key elements of the criminal justice system entangles restorative justice in aporias that differentiate by holding firmly onto, even hypostatising, identities and concepts of the very paradigm it seeks to surpass. The chapter explores several unintended consequences for governmentalities that oblige subjects to be victims of crime.

In addition, the *imitor* paradox is renewed by the way in which restorative governmentalities use their approach to offenders as a marker of differentiation from retributive approaches. The ultimate aim is to help offenders reintegrate into communities. Chapter 4 explores how the attempt to differentiate restorative governmentalities from the abstracted coercions of courtroom justice collapses by assuming the identity of an individual offender who has committed a crime – as defined by the courtroom. Notwithstanding important restrictions that this imposes on possible visions of harm, the assumption of juridical definitions of crime, and an emphasis on individual offenders, commits restorative justice to key tenets of the adversarial mentalities it claims to exceed.

In a related fashion, Chapter 5 analyses the *imitor* paradox as it surfaces in restorative claims to mobilise an amorphous 'community' that differentiates community-based from state-based justice. Despite wide variation in how they define the concept, restorative governmentalities predicate their images of community on the commission of a crime, and further require the active participation of victims and offenders to achieve community strength. Again, the aporetic structure of the *imitor* finds advocates alleging difference on the basis of precepts defined and central to that which is to be exceeded. The final chapter, Chapter 6, works with openings implied by the previous analyses of the paradox at hand to contemplate the promise of justice in excess of current meaning horizons and practices.

Insinuations

The impulse to be both alternative and appendage is highlighted, and indeed supported, by the ambiguities of claiming to provide a radically different framework of values that are *not* entirely absent from the criminal justice system. This enables restorative justice advocates to make syntactically meaningful claims to alternative processes without – and this is important – jettisoning a profound, even fundamental, attachment to criminal justice. It allows restorative justice to be absorbed as complement into its supposed opposite. There are, as we shall see, important political benefits to maintaining the paradoxical stance in a climate which emphasises 'cultures of crime' while attacking the welfare state. However, the paradox does enable us to think carefully about what it may mean to attempt calculations of justice beyond both restorative and criminal visions of justice.

One could draw these introductory discussions to a provisional close by referring to the intentional ambiguity of the book's title. 'Governing paradoxes' connotes either paradoxes that rule over something, or the idea of governing through paradox. Both apply to the terrain sketched out in this introductory chapter. In the silent caverns of unspoken assumption that forge restorative governmentalities, I have outlined how paradox rules over rich dominions of value and process, over political logics that render practicable techniques like conferencing, mediation and conciliation. Simultaneously, and not unrelated to that reflection, there is an equally significant effect: restorative governance is largely accomplished through paradoxical rejections of and commitments to state criminal justice. Governing through the *imitor* paradox has become so familiar a *modus operandi* that it seldom courts a second glance; what follows reflectively explores the contours of that paradox, looking at its impossible structure for glimpses into what may be – in our times – an unconquerable feature of pursuing justice in excess of law.

Chapter 2
Healing Crime's Harm

Since restorative governmentalities distinguish themselves from retributive approaches by appealing to different traditions and moral frameworks of justice, we are exhorted to adopt different moral frameworks of intelligibility. New conceptual lenses will, so the reasoning goes, allow us to replace an emphasis on retribution, coercion, guilt and punishment with one directed at healing the harms of criminal acts and repairing the damage caused (Zehr, 1990). Restorative justice also focuses on recovering victim voices as key definers of contextual harms, requires offenders to take responsibility for generating that harm, and expects communities to become actively involved in restitutively resolving the situation (see Johnstone, 2003). Allied values are espoused as pivotal: restoration, compassion, forgiveness, redemption, reparation, reintegration, empowerment, self-determination, respect, voluntarism, community strength, participation, peacemaking, harmony, and so on.[1]

The enunciation of this grouped set of values is clearly meant to signal a discrete break from the different traditions and moral compass of the adversarial criminal justice system and its punishment regimes. At the same time, however, by positioning its value framework as contingent upon crime, as working in the aftermath of crime, restorative justice paradoxically commits itself to the very moral framework it claims to supplant. This paradoxical commitment has several implications in context, and it is to such matters that I now turn.

---

1   For example, see Braithwaite (2002), Zehr (2002) and Johnstone (2002).

Different traditions of justice

Restorative justice is said to descend from ancient traditions of justice, far older than relatively recent state-based traditions (see Johnstone, 2002). Here, it has to be said that some bold historical claims are made. For example, Braithwaite maintains that:

> ... restorative justice has been the dominant model of criminal justice throughout most of human history for all the world's peoples (2002: 5).

Its approach, we are told, is embedded:

> ... in traditions of justice from the ancient Arab, Greek, and Roman civilizations but even in 'Indian Hindu' traditions dating to 6000–2000 BC (1999: 1).

Equally audacious is Consedine's (1995) analysis of biblical justice as essentially restorative in nature. Weitekamp's more detailed 'history of restorative justice' draws on an 'abundant literature' on 'primitive acephalous societies' to indicate the longstanding centrality of restorative justice traditions throughout human history, and the relatively rare reliance on retributive punishments (2003: 14). His conclusion is unequivocal:

> ... humans have used forms of restorative justice for the larger part of their existence. Penal law and the often destructive retributive answer to crime – or, more recently, the failed rehabilitative efforts – have been fairly new (2003: 122).

Evidently, at its most grandiose, restorative justice discourse differentiates itself by claiming a distinct and ancient lineage, viewed as quite separate from that of state criminal justice, which – in this wider compass – is deemed to be a recent invention that takes root with the gradual erosion of restorative approaches from roughly the 12th century onwards (Weitekamp, 2003). Disaggregating the broad picture, the larger claim is that restorative traditions predate legal justice systems and that 'nonjudicial' and 'nonlegal' techniques for resolving disputes have dominated the West's past (Zehr, 2003, 1990). For most of that history, the state is said to have played a relatively minimal role in dealing with crime and bringing prosecutions before resolution tribunals. Over the past several centuries, however, both state and church (eg, through inquisitions) have become more involved in instigating prosecutions, with the state secularising canon law and adopting common law models of inquisition and accusation.

Zehr interprets these developments in this way:

> ... history has been a dialectic between two rival systems. Community justice was basically extra-legal, often negotiated, often restitutive. State justice was legal, expressing formal rationalism and rules, the rigidification of custom and principles derived from the Roman tradition into law. It was imposed justice, punitive justice, hierarchical justice (in Johnstone, 2003: 76).

He adds further that the rise of capitalism, nation states and the 'breakdown of communities' become key influences in the attrition of restorative justice traditions and nourish the eventual dominance of the state's criminal justice system.

These historical visions posit the rise of retributive criminal justice as coterminous with the emergence of administrative, centralised state formations that absorb the function of responding to crime -- previously this fell to victims and affected communities. Over time, the state's justice system defines crime as an 'offence against the state' (Zehr, 2003: 72). One could rightly challenge, as does Daly (2003b) from within the restorative justice thematic, these somewhat extraordinary claims, and indeed whether such a diverse assemblage of times/places could ever constitute anything like a unified 'tradition', let alone a 'restorative' one.

Through such accounts, criminal justice traditions are regarded as essentially retributive, punitive, violent, adversarial, rule-bound, formal (thus rigid and unresponsive), coercive and guilt-centred (Umbreit, 2001). The legacy of this justice is one in which the victim and community are sidelined as professionals, and state agents, together with combative accusatorial processes, become central to the administration of justice. By contrast, restorative justice is posited as an attempt to revitalise older traditions of justice by championing the plight of victims and communities while holding offenders directly accountable in non-retributive ways (Umbreit, 2001: xxxviii). That is, the aim is to return to a previous emphasis on the role of victims and communities when dealing with crime.

A (re-)valued lens

By claiming to be a contemporary expression of an ancient tradition of justice, restorative governmentalities evoke an alternative framework of values.[2] Hence, Braithwaite and Strang note that:

> ... it is values that distinguish restorative justice from traditional punitive state justice. Restorative justice is about healing (restoration) rather than hurting. Responding to the hurt of crime with the hurt of punishment is rejected, along with its corresponding value of proportionality – punishment that is proportionate to the wrong that has been done. The idea is that the value of healing is key because the crucial dynamic to foster is healing that begets healing (Strang and Braithwaite, 2001: 1–2).

So, where state systems of justice are portrayed as operating around retributive *values* in their image and practice of justice, restorative justice advocates offer a different moral scheme that emphasises *healing the harms produced by crime*.[3] Here, justice is conceptualised around notions of healing harm, 'restoring right relations' and 'reconciling' stakeholders. As Graef puts it, 'Restorative justice means just what it says: restoring the balance of the situation disturbed by crime or conflict, and making good the harm caused to the individuals concerned' (2001: 11). This focus on healing harms is contrasted with criminal justice emphases on punishing or rehabilitating individual offenders.[4] Therefore:

---

2 See especially Johnstone (2003) and Daly (2003b), but also Johnstone (2002), Sharpe (1998) and Zehr (1990).

3 Specifically, as noted in passing, state criminal justice is said to centre on retributive values that ground a general emphasis on blame, accusation, wrongdoing, guilt, the rule of law, repression, abstracted rules, coercion, deterrence, proportionate punishment, 'an eye for an eye', stigma and sometimes rehabilitation (Zehr, 2003; 1997). In turn, such values lie behind judgmental, adversarial, accusatorial and rule-bound practices enacted at courthouses around the world. These practices focus on abstract questions of guilt in relation to statutory codes, and are directed primarily towards offenders. Allied with the values and focus of retributive systems of justice is an emphasis on developing sufficiently severe punishments to serve as both specific and general deterrents to future offending.

4 Umbreit puts it thus: 'Restorative justice is based on values that emphasize the importance of providing more active support and assistance to crime victims; holding offenders directly accountable to the people and communities they have violated; restoring the emotional and material losses of victims as much as possible; providing a range of opportunities for dialogue and problem solving among interested crime victims, offenders, families, and other support persons; offering offenders opportunities for competency development and reintegration into productive community life; and strengthening public safety through community building' (Umbreit, 2001: xxxvii–xxxviii).

A just response to crime must not only correct the offending behavior, but also address the harm done by that behaviour – both to the primary victims and to the community (Sharpe, 1998: 46).

The overall shift in values leads restorative justice advocates to a particular rationale: crime causes a breach in 'right relations' between people, produces interactive ills, assaults the harmony of a collective whole (community), produces material and emotional devastation, and so leaves a trail of harm in its wake. Restorative justice is specifically directed to dealing with the various contours of that harm (especially as defined by victims and community) through ameliorative restorative processes (eg, community mediation, victim-offender mediation, family group conferences, etc). As such, justice is less about punishing people and more about achieving a presumed relational equilibrium. Let us turn to restorative visions of harm and healing in more detail.

Visions of harm

Restorative governmentalities envisage crime as intrinsically harm-producing and this approach renders practicable the idea that restorative practices ought to focus on individual or communal harms produced by crime. It is through 'harm' that 'criminal action' is presented as something that occurs between real, live people (as opposed to abstracted legal persons). Harm materialises as well as tangibly expresses what is most significant about a criminal event, and this is why restorative justice focuses its attention on criminal harm.[5] As Sharpe puts it:

Thus the starting place in restorative justice is not breaking the law, but the harm done when crime is committed ... the damage may be tangible or emotional, limited or extensive, brief or long-lasting. In any case, something has been lost, harmed or broken, to the detriment of individual lives. A restorative perspective is concerned with that detriment, and believes justice must somehow address the harm (1998: 8).

---

5 Restorative justice advocates argue that the criminal justice system fails to recognise this basic point, and so – *inter alia* – makes the mistake of overlooking the victim's plight: 'What gets lost in such a system, however, is the reality that crime involves much more than breaking rules. Crime involves real actions that hurt real people, with real and lasting consequences. But a justice system bent on catching and punishing criminals has little to offer victims of crime' (Sharpe, 1998: 3).

Since its focus is on 'real people' and their lives, restorative justice is far less concerned with abstracted legal rules than it is 'with people in their communities in the aftermath of crime' (Graef, 2001: 9).

But how exactly do restorative moral frameworks of justice approach the harm produced by crime? For the most part, the discourse evokes words such as 'damage', 'hurt', 'broken', 'loss', and so on, to explain the meaning of harm. Such harms may be material, physical, emotional, and relational. However, there are three important observations to make in this regard.

First, restorative justice advocates accept that there are multiple and diverse manifestations of harm, depending on the crime, the context and the participants. As such, the discourse does not proffer a universal vision of the damage caused by crime, arguing instead that there are many possible configurations thereof. Restorative justice recognises the contextually-specific nature of the meanings attributed to criminal actions, and that this has an impact on the perception or definitions of harm for participants. So, for example, one victim may regard the theft of his or her motor car philosophically as a redistribution of wealth; another materially well-off victim might see it as an unexpected opportunity to purchase another vehicle; a solo parent victim who depends fundamentally on the vehicle may experience serious hardship in consequence; another might perceive the theft as a elemental intrusion, or violation, and be terrified by the incident. In each case, the harm associated with the criminal action differs, and so leads to qualitatively different experiences for those involved. Thus, the category of harm, being sensitive to varieties of situation and subject, is also highly malleable.

This leads to the second and crucial point. Since harm is contextually defined, affected participants *are required to articulate* through restorative processes their sense of being harmed in specific contexts and in relation to particular events. Victims must specify its precise form in a given context (Braithwaite and Mugford, 1994). This explains why restorative justice processes, such as mediation, are explicitly designed to bring victims, offenders and community to face-to-face meetings that give everyone (especially the victim) the opportunity to negotiate and define the contours of the harm or harms that are involved in and emanate from a given criminal event (eg, Umbreit, 2001: Chapter 3). In aiming to empower victims and others to narrate such contours as they see it – to reclaim ownership of the trauma as it were (Christie, 1977) – the articulation of harm is placed as a key focus for restorative visions of justice.

Thirdly, the discourse argues that harm generates specific *needs* in those affected by crime (Zehr, 1990). Restorative justice is designed to address these needs by empowering participants to articulate the precise shape of need in context (for example, victims might need to be reassured that the event was random, or to express their anger towards offenders, etc). It should also allow participants (notably, victims, offenders and the community) to negotiate how to meet those needs (Johnstone, 2002: 62 ff).

Thus, the proposed moral framework of restorative justice does not precisely define abstract principles of harm; rather it promotes the need for processes that allow affected victims, offenders and community members to define its perceived contours in a given context. Crime is the *a priori* wrong; harm emerges as a result of that wrong. Restorative visions construe justice as a way of dealing with harms that constitute the aftermath of crime.

Healing the restorative way

> If crime is injury, justice will repair injuries and promote healing. Acts of restoration will … counterbalance the harm of crime. We cannot guarantee full recovery … but true justice would aim to promote a context in which the process can occur (Zehr, 1990: 9).

The emphasis on healing, restoring and repairing reflects the key remedial responses that restorative frameworks of justice deem appropriate to redressing the needs generated by harm. Several issues are associated with such moral frameworks of restorative healing. First, the concept of healing licences specific governmental techniques such as conferencing and mediation. These techniques are supposed to:

- enable victims, offenders and members of the affected community to define the nature of harm surrounding a specific criminal act;
- enunciate and validate the needs generated by harm as defined by the respective parties;
- emphasise the needs of the victim;
- afford opportunities for offenders to make meaningful amends, to be treated with respect and yet be positively

shamed in preparation for reintegration into the community; and

- address communal needs (eg, fear, anger, etc) by rebuilding the broken fabric of community that both nurtures and is affected by crime.

Healing in this sense involves meaningfully addressing contextually defined needs following a crime. The various restorative justice processes (eg, family group conferences, community mediation, community panels) are designed to reach a consensus: victims (typically) are required to speak for themselves, while offenders are required to listen, understand, recognise the harm caused, apologise, and suggest how to redress their offending behaviour. Community representatives are also invited to have a say in how the crime has affected them. Using negotiation, conciliation, mediation and other forms of 'community' dialogue, all parties are encouraged to express their needs, and to help generate plans that will allow them to 'move on' (Sharpe, 1998: 8).

Secondly, the notion of healing is meant to be a future-orientated gesture insofar as it tries to rectify, to the greatest possible extent, the harm of a past criminal event. The point of dealing with needs arising from such harm is to ensure that all participants get on with their lives to the best possible degree. Offenders are also sometimes required to undergo rituals of redemption, such as 'positive' shaming, in a bid to reintegrate them into a community (Braithwaite, 1989). Feelings of shame in offenders could be mobilised to generate sincere apologies and a willingness to make meaningful amends. Such shaming could also be used to encourage offenders to seek out ways to alter offending identities (eg, through counselling) and to reintegrate them into communities. The purpose of restorative healing is to devise problem-solving strategies to enable all the participants and affected others to move beyond the criminal event. The emphasis is on finding ways to repair, heal and restore breaches to individuals, relations and a presumed harmonious, communal whole.

Thirdly, for the most part, restorative justice advocates feel that a community 'owns' the crime and conflict in its midst, and so must be directly involved with, and take responsibility for, addressing the relational ruptures it creates (Christie, 1977; Sharpe, 1998: 47). However, as detailed in Chapter 5, there are at least two important images of 'community responsibility' and how best to address the 'needs' of the community in context. On the one hand, community responsibility is taken by many to mean effectively redressing the needs created by crime and restoring an assumed *trust* broken by a criminal act. Community responsibility is here defined as the need for a community to deal with the aftermath of crime, and to ensure that the community becomes (or remains) a safe, secure and collectively meaningful space for all members. The main objective is to restore a community's fabric by dealing effectively with victims' needs, successfully reintegrating offenders, and building community strength by requiring communities to deal with the criminal event through restorative processes.

On the other hand, some advocates define community responsibility thus: contemporary communities, by virtue of their structure, create opportunities, identities and incitements for people to commit crime. This communitarian bent within restorative justice discourse calls for processes to heal broken relations between people to reduce crime and build viable communities.[6] For example, Morris calls for transformative justice processes that:

> ... enable the wider community to take responsibility for the underlying causes of crime: poverty, abused children, unemployment, discrimination, and other deep social problems. The community is enabled to take these on in digestible servings. It does not need to solve the whole unemployment poverty problem at once, but each case dealt with transformatively enables the community to work on a portion of it, contribute to its healing, and understand and address better the larger issues that lie behind it. Transformative justice processes are the building blocks of an informed, concerned, and healthy community, one that cares for and includes all of its members (2000: 254).

Equally, Bush and Folger (1994) call for mediation to actualise its potential ability to change community relations. This approach challenges notions that healing must be conservatively 'restorative' in the sense of 'restoring' an existing status quo. A key point raised here is that certain communities are in and of themselves criminogenic, and to restore relations in such environments is to set the conditions for increased criminal

---

6 See Pavlich (2001) for more on communitarian approaches to restorative justice.

behaviour. With this is mind, one can better see why some communitarians call for transformative, as opposed to strictly restorative, justice; for them, healing involves changing problematic communal relations as much as satisfying individual need.

One final point on healing: restorative justice advocates differentiate their formulations from more positivist-inspired rehabilitation frameworks within criminal justice system orientations. The latter's visions of healing are aligned with the 'therapeutic' treatments of conservative Western medicine. For example, Johnstone (2002: 94–95) argues that rehabilitative treatment fails because criminals are encouraged by the therapeutic paradigm to see themselves as the product of a pre-determined nature (ie, the notion that people become criminals because of biological or psychological predispositions).[7] Such paradigms enable (sometimes even encourage) offenders to adopt a passive role in their own rehabilitation, and do not require them to take responsibility for their actions.

By contrast, restorative justice appeals to more holistic visions of healing and conveys a less formal, open-minded, responsive set of interventions. It aims to ensure that offenders are confronted with 'moral judgments of their behaviour if they are to come to an understanding of the harm they have caused and of their liability to repair it' (Johnstone, 2002: 94–95). Healing in restorative justice is thus focused on taking responsibility and making things right, restoring right relations between people. Further, as Bazemore (1998) notes, the process of healing ought not to focus on offenders at the expense of victims. Both victims and offenders should become active participants in the healing processes; restorative justice is designed to create forums within which both can accomplish this. [8]

Harm, healing and the *imitor* paradox

The concept of restoration is associated with values like wholeness, harmony, peace, health, reparation, restitution,

---

7 See Pfohl (1994) for a lucid discussion of this positivist approach or, as he terms it, the 'pathological perspective'.

8 Braithwaite's modest assessment here is that while restorative justice has a 'better theory of rehabilitation than the welfare model provides' (2002: 73), it is not currently having much success in rehabilitating offenders on the ground; however, he feels it provides the auspices for that to occur (2002: 96–102).

reintegration and restoration.[9] In context, as we have seen, restorative governmentalities prescribe a change of moral lens: doing justice involves dealing with the harmful *aftermath* of crime. Healing presupposes a harm and restorative governmentalities' definitions of harm are predicated on prior, legal definitions of 'crime'. Because restorative justice processes are directed to the 'aftermath of crime', they thereby do not actually contest the law's right to define crime, but merely broaden it. For all intents and purposes, restorative justice's claimed opposition to criminal justice, and its claims to offer an alternative, are parasitic upon legally defined crimes. Restorative justice thus conceptually and practically subordinates itself to the very criminal justice system it claims to escape. Hence, the *imitor* paradox appears in perhaps the most fundamental gesture of restorative justice: its claim to heal. The attempt to change moral lenses from criminal to restorative justice turns out paradoxically to hinge on a notion of healing that is predicated on a defining feature of criminal justice: crime as the basis of harm. The restorative quest for a different moral framework of justice grounds itself in the very value orientation it seeks to redress.

At the same time, as fleetingly indicated, this moral framework implicitly appeals to a medical model that – again paradoxically – has the effect of masking ethical decisions as technical necessities. For example, so long as one sees the task of justice as healing the harms of crime, there is no need to engage the ethical question of whether harm may exist outside of 'crime', or perhaps even whether certain definitions of crime are themselves harmful (see below). By focusing on *healing* the harms generated by crime, restorative justice rhetorically appeals to a medical model that takes for granted several fundamental concepts defined by the criminal justice system. In pursuit of restoring a 'healthy' equilibrium, measures to heal the breaches of crime are brought into play with the intention of restoring relational balances.[10] The appeal to a medical model significantly restricts the ways that justice can be conceptualised, and tends to

---

9 See, eg, Johnstone (2003) and Walgrave (2002b).

10 One thinks analogously of a healthy body being ripped open through trauma, and the race to a hospital, where medical practitioners perform healing measures that diagnose, treat and stabilise the harmed body in an effort to restore the body back to a healthy, even if somewhat scarred, state.

focus restorative discussions on diagnosing conditions, restoring a presumed healthy order and the healer who attends to both these matters.[11] This appeal also enables the *imitor* paradox to surface because restorative justice thereby predicates its diagnoses, orders and healer identities on legal definitions of crime.

Crime, diagnosis and harm

If restorative diagnoses centre on notions of harm generated by crime, the governmentality encourages victims, offenders and affected community members to define the contours of that harm (eg, through conferencing, mediation, etc). However, as noted, crime is assumed to be primordial to, and the instigator of, the harm to which restorative diagnoses and healing are directed. As such, crime is the primary breach of a healthy condition, and that disruption surfaces, symptomatically perhaps, as harms which generate particular needs in victims, offenders and communities. Restorative justice aims to help participants define that harm, but crime remains in the background as the primary event whose aftermath is claimed by restorative justice.

But how do restorative justice advocates define crime? This question touches on one of the embedded secrets of restorative justice governmentalities, an aspect of the assumptive universe that grounds restorative discourses: no fully-fledged alternative definitions of, or even ways of defining, crime are provided. For all practical purposes, proponents accept that crime is defined by law and its criminal justice system. This is the bedrock upon which restorative justice stands. Chapter 4 deals with this matter

---

11 Specifically, when grafted onto restorative justice contexts, the medical model is predicated on at least three key assumptions: (1) normal, ordered and healthy social relations exist between people, and restorative justice restores the disrupted order to approximations of its former healthy state; (2) crime is diagnosed as a disease that attacks the integrity of healthy relationships and the trauma generates harm/needs; and (3) restorative justice processes provide the healer and medicine to heal the harms produced in the aftermath of crime. Several questions arise when considering the appropriation of the medical model: is it apposite to borrow the assumptions of this model and graft it onto a very differently composed social field? Equally, why would one want to appropriate a naïve version of that model, one that is widely understood to be politically charged, whose technical appearance masks an underlying nest of assumed values and whose privileged position is seriously challenged within medical fields?

in more detail; suffice here to note that even with vague attempts to posit crime as a violation or disruption of relations between people (Zehr, 2002: 21), we are left pondering how such unclear formulations could replace legal definitions. All the focus on harm does little to transcend criminal law, which stands as a background colossus to the relative tinkering of restorative enunciations of harm and need.[12] The basic discursive apparatus of restorative governmentalities revolves around concepts which are no different from, and indeed have been defined by, those which ground the criminal justice system.

If such insights allude again to restorative justice's paradoxical claims to being a fundamental alternative to the criminal justice system whose founding concepts it assumes as given, they also suggest a very narrow range of possible diagnoses of harm in a given set of circumstances.

Restoring what?

Without clearly redefining crime, restorative justice discourses presume the presence of a communally ordered, 'healthy' relational state. Etymologically, the word 'health' and its verb, 'heal', refer to the 'state of being whole' (Ayto, 1990: 277). 'Health', 'heal', 'whole' and several related words derive from the prehistoric Germanic word *khailas* meaning 'undamaged' (Ayto, 1990: 573). An assumption of wholeness, health, order and purity is necessary for restorative justice advocates to claim that harm is generated by a particular cause (crime), and that a particular remedy or pattern of healing can redress harm and restore harmony to the whole. Within restorative justice governmentalities, there are several formulations of precisely what relational health or wholeness might entail, but let us here consider two influential versions.

First, as noted above, Zehr takes crime to be a violation of people's identities which is devastating because:

> ... it upsets two fundamental assumptions on which we base our lives: our belief that the world is an orderly, meaningful place, and our belief in personal autonomy. Both assumptions are essential for wholeness (1990: 24).

---

12 Equally dependent upon dominant criminal justice system approaches to crime is the way in which restorative diagnoses rely fundamentally on notions of the victim and offender.

Thus, for human beings to achieve a state of wholeness, of health, they must *believe* that the world is ordered around personal autonomy. If they do not possess such beliefs, by implication, they cannot achieve a state of wholeness. The point applies as much to offenders as it does to victims.

For victims, the violations of criminality dissolve their sense of health and wholeness by shattering the beliefs that order their lives. They suffer the effects of the devastation, giving rise to feelings of fear, violation and mistrust. Offenders, by virtue of their criminal behaviour, tangibly express the breakdown in these beliefs: they certainly have not accepted the social world as a fundamentally consensual, orderly and meaningful place. Nor have they respected personal autonomy – otherwise they would have respected an implicit social contract that protects those whose autonomy they have violated. From this point of view, the most fundamental harm of crime is precisely that it challenges both of these belief systems, by challenging existing legal orders and violating notions of personal autonomy. As such, healing involves restoring these fundamental beliefs.

In the second version, images of health cluster around a strong community. We will return to this in Chapter 5, but the emphasis on community – even if differently understood – suggests a unified, functioning, harmonious, empowered, democratic, accommodating, inclusive, connected, consensual and unified whole. This picture of health is violated by criminal behaviour; restorative justice is mobilised as a way to heal such violations through community-based processes that include individually-focused mediations, somewhat broader relational conferencing and wider transformative configurations. The entire mentality of governance, the ways of seeing which render particular kinds of governing practicable, is therefore premised upon the idea that there is an ideal state of community that symbolises health, harmony, balance and so on.

Both these notions of health indicate how restorative mentalities predicate themselves on assumptions of an ideal and healthy state of being with others; the task of any justice process is to preserve that order and restore any given (fallen?) condition to that presumed ideal. If social health is equated with a consensual order, relational wholeness is only ever possible in the absence of legally defined crime, and here again we see a prior attachment to criminal justice. Moreover, the presupposition of an ordered unity is grounded upon some troubling notions of purity that belie assumptions of health and order.

Bauman offers an interesting interpretation of this uniquely modern 'dream of purity' that enables assumptions of wholeness, and is not unrelated to eugenic quests to erect variously defined 'pure' societies. As he puts it, 'Purity is an ideal; a vision of the condition which needs yet to be created, or such as needs to be diligently protected against the genuine or imagined odds' (1997: 5). And the idealised order suggests that:

> ... each thing is in its rightful place and nowhere else ... 'Order' means a regular, stable environment for our action; a world in which the probabilities of events on not distributed at random, but arranged in a strict hierarchy (1997: 6–7).

Harm is the friend – the outcome – of disorder and the enemy of order. Such a sensibility is certainly not outside the remit of restorative justice governmentalities, and indeed the idea that justice could be reclaimed to deploy this ideal state of self-worth, moral progress, justice and communality is very much part of the discourses around harm and order.

The question that then emerges is what sort of justice might be imagined through such thinking and, perhaps more importantly, what possibilities for justice are left out when one makes the assumption that there is an ideal social world, circumscribed by legal definitions of crime, to which the fallen may again aspire? Here, restorative justice governmentalities betray a paradoxical commitment to legally endorsed visions of order and wholeness (health), which connotes a degree of determinacy about the contexts under scrutiny; *at the same time* they call for open and negotiated designations of harm and its contextually-defined redress. This paradoxical commitment to order *and* openness, determinacy *and* indeterminacy, decidability *and* undecidability, stasis *and* dynamism etc indicates the ambivalence surrounding restorative calculations of justice. On the one hand, restorative justice eschews the formal, rule-bound nature of law, but yet defers to formulations of wholeness that are supported by law's designations of crime. On the other, it calculates justice as an informal, negotiated, context specific matter but then it seeks restoration to an order without questioning whether that order may itself – under certain circumstances – be criminogenic.

Restorative justice and the parasitical healer

In response to the needs created by the harms of crime, restorative justice's moral framework suggests images of a healer who understands that crime involves a transgression of right relations between people, and that it will often have raw emotional elements. In the aftermath of crime, harm releases relational, material and emotional needs in victims, offenders and affected community members. The restorative healer is an architect of mediation environments that aim to let participants define how they have been harmed by a crime and what needs it has generated for them. Then, the astute healer seeks to address such needs.

Two observations regarding the healer suggest ways in which the *imitor* paradox is replicated. First, the healer is mostly conceived as an individual person who operates within a process that pledges allegiance to restorative principles. In addition, given the mammoth task of relational restoration following a crime, the healer would seem to possess almost mystical powers capable of addressing the needs of all affected parties. But the restorative justice healer is never called upon to exercise these powers because it is a subaltern figure within a broader criminal justice mandate. The healer is parasitically reliant upon criminal justice for designations of crime and becomes effective in helping participants to translate crime into vocabularies of harm, need and satisfactory expiation. The healer solicits from participants personally meaningful accounts about the harm of a criminal event and then helps them to translate such narratives into expressions of need. Thereafter, the needs are interpreted so as to render them amenable to concrete redress and resolution. Through this sequence of events, one glimpses the extent to which the identity of this healer is parasitic upon a criminal justice system whose designation of crime plays host to subsequent restorative processes.

Secondly, the question of neutrality often raised in context is a red herring. Even in those circumstances where the healer remains relatively impartial with respect to participants' narratives, he or she has already committed to fundamental concepts underlying criminal justice formulations. In other words, for example, the healer may impartially elicit needs within a family group conference from confessors, and may even be agnostic as to which means should be used to address these needs. However, by focusing on narratives that originate from a 'crime', the healer commits in advance to key values of the criminal justice system. Ironically, by claiming neutrality in a given set of circumstances, the healer distracts attention away from a prior, more fundamental attachment to legal discourses of crime and order.

Justice, ethics and the clinical

Because restorative governmentalities are implicitly framed within a medical model, despite supporters' claims to work within different moral frameworks, restorative justice effectively quietens discussion on the ethical dimensions of justice. In so doing, the discourse is not well positioned to challenge, fundamentally, the ethical values of criminal justice that supporters claim to surpass. How so? In general terms, the medical model implies a clinical, or technical, resolution to a given trauma; ie, a harrowing situation is determined and explainable by natural laws that may be manipulated and managed to regain 'health'. This is quite different from recognising the fundamental openness and indeterminacy of everyday life that -- precisely because it is not determined -- makes ethics possible, and calculations, or negotiations, of justice essentially open-ended. One might even say that the implicit reliance on medical analogies in restorative governmentalities betrays what was most promising about its early formulations: its opening up to undetermined, ethical possibilities of justice in local contexts.

In any case, the technical language of the medical analogy should be treated with extreme caution because it masks fundamental ethical questions involved in framing justice around images of health, wholeness and collective integrity. If this issue is complicated enough in medical domains, it is arguably more vexed when one applies the idea of wholeness to communities or social collectives. When the model is imported into the context of restorative justice, many thorny moral, social and political conundrums are conveniently silenced in favour of technicist blueprints that become standard fare for many restorative calculations of justice.

The medical model may be useful for some, since it connotes a semblance of 'pure science', objectivity, empirical rigor, beneficent care and an ability to increase overall health. Additionally, it translates contingent moral decisions into a technical language that has the appearance of being necessary -- it has the ability to wrest from complex social relations demarcated and manageable problems that lend themselves to resolution through effective healing and treatment. This technical language has proved enormously effective in silencing the inevitable undecidable character that comprises legitimate domains of ethics, which come into operation precisely because areas of human life are undetermined (Pavlich, 2002a). That is, medical model languages effectively translate irrevocable moral dilemmas into technically resolvable problems. The upshot is this: so long as restorative justice embraces a medical model approach to justice, it embeds its governmentalities within managerial, administrative discourses at the expense of ethical discussions more appropriate to questions of justice.

In turn, this radically limits its supporters' promise to pursue justice through an alternative ethical framework of values, and inordinately narrows the scope of their attempts to rekindle a different tradition of justice. Furthermore, by predicating its narratives of harm on criminal justice definitions of crime, and seeking to restore a taken-for-granted order through the identity of healers parasitically dependent on crime discourses, restorative justice relies fundamentally on the very value framework it claims to exceed. Its implicit reliance on a medical model, in addition, does not enable focused *ethical* challenges to criminal justice horizons. As a result, the espoused attempts to find ethical values that surpass criminal justice arenas are muted by a paradoxical commitment to those arenas' conceptual foundations.

Chapter 3
Victims of Restorative Governmentalities

For some decades now, the victim has been ensconced as a central figure in Western cultures, especially in crime-related arenas. A Young's (1996) insightful deconstruction of the broad discursive resources used to sustain notions of 'crime' and associated 'victims' illustrates the degree to which these concepts are entwined with one another and indeed contemporary visions of citizenship. Criminal justice arenas now also place renewed emphasis on victims (for example, victim rights and victim support movements), and there is a well-established discipline of victimology specifically directed to the study of crime victims.[1] Such developments have helped to erect, sustain and advance conditions that expressly champion victim identities, and restorative justice's emphasis on victim-centred processes adds a specific dimension to that ethos.

To speculate somewhat, this established focus on victims may be related to a broad decline in beliefs that universal reason is sufficiently fixed to secure social progress (Bauman, 1992, 1997). That was, after all, one of the favoured Enlightenment dreams, where modern disciplines promised to divine secular but ahistorical points of reference – yardsticks – for guiding the way to progress. Without stable beliefs in a universally held yardstick to guide human endeavours, without a sense that such a common telos might exist, advanced liberal images of tolerance and diversity have flourished (MacIntyre, 1988; Lyotard and Thébaud, 1985). The idea that reason could provide a single, foundational unity to direct progressive societies is challenged by radically different visions of what it is to live life in accord with reason (see Lyotard, 1984). Added to this, one should not forget that the gas chambers, the cruelties of Apartheid, Stalin's purges,

---

1   See, eg, Doerner and Lab (1998), Rock (1994) and Walklate (1989).

and world wars all claimed to be under some or other spell of reason. Indeed, the Frankfurt School and Bauman's variations note the degree to which modern reason provided the enabling conditions for such atrocities. The sheer scale of the past century's historical disasters has challenged whatever comfort is to be gained by declaring that reason is sufficient to guarantee social advancement.

Consequently, many people find themselves drifting without a collectively held sense of how exactly to be with others, pondering with disquiet the uncertain currents of a socially splintered diversity that threatens to dissolve any sense of common unity. This has, perhaps, intensified a search for secure footings from which to approach everyday life, and has conferred a certain privilege to victim narratives, especially the emotionally charged first-person accounts of those who have suffered. The empathic sway of voices that tell of sacrifice and suffering at the hands of others, confessing their tales with riveting frankness, is particularly influential in ethical contexts marked by a pervasive uncertainty (Bauman, 1992, 1994). Exacting a basic empathy with the other, and thereby affirming a collective unity beyond everyday self interest, is precisely the province of victim narratives. The privilege accorded to such narratives allows us to reaffirm that we humans are, despite the diversity, fundamentally connected. Without any comforting agreement on independent, universal moral yardsticks, the many can still experience collective oneness, joined by experiences of sympathy with, empathy towards and perhaps an understanding of a victim's plight.

In this ethos, a complex politics of victim and victimisation has produced new social processes that appear very much like modern day confessionals, championing the voices of victims, offering them new domains, therapies and incitements to speak (Furedi, 2004). One thinks of the many rituals and techniques designed to exact narratives from those who have suffered: before hordes of counsellors, the gaze of millions enraptured by Oprah Winfrey-type TV shows, the avid readers of mass-produced books. Rituals that oblige the formation and presence of victims are no longer the preserve of experts; rather, techniques for producing victim identities have been generalised to many areas of the social fabric. The previous chapter has already referred to the translation techniques used to reframe criminal harm into the language of victim (and other) needs in restorative justice contexts. Such techniques supply, nurture and legitimate the routines and performances by which subjects emerge as full-bodied victims – their narratives ground new organisations of truth, taking hold where once modernity's reason-ensconced experts held primary sway.

Restorative justice has located itself at the heart of a politics of how to treat crime victims, offering its various techniques and practices as venues for 'victims' to narrate and interpret images of themselves in relation to a criminal event. Restorative governmentalities claim thereby to 'empower' such victims, allowing them to identify 'needs' (as victims), and to have a significant voice in the conferences, mediations, sentencing circles, etc, designed to address those needs.

This chapter explores dominant conceptions of the 'victim' in restorative governmentalities, before considering how the latter seek to govern subjects through notions of the empowered victim. I use as a framing example guidelines enunciated by Umbreit (2001) on how to practise victim-offender mediation to examine the manner in which subjects are obliged to identify as particular sorts of victims in order to participate in restorative justice processes. In effect, restorative justice governs by facilitating and producing particular kinds of victim identities. In this context, the *imitor* paradox surfaces insofar as restorative justice seeks to distinguish itself from criminal justice systems by emphasising victim participation in its processes. However, by positing the victim identity as central to such processes, restorative governmentalities are predicated on an identity that is generated, in the first instance at least, by admissions of guilt within criminal justice arenas.[2]

It will be argued that there are at least two related implications of this paradox. First, the claim to empower victims *as victims* is problematic when one considers that by definition the 'victim' is a disempowered identity, connoting suffering at the hands of another. In consequence, restorative images of justice emerge as

---

2　For those inclined to argue that the criminal justice system has complainants rather than victims *per se*, we should recall that restorative justice techniques operate on the premise of guilt admission which – in criminal law – is deemed *ipso facto* to generate victims. Crime and victim go hand in hand within criminal justice discourses – even if the state itself is sometimes designated that role. Restorative justice is usually mobilised in specific cases where individual victims are identified as products of a legally-defined criminal offence. That image of victimhood underpins restorative governmentalities.

direct homologies, rather than alternatives, to the calculations of the criminal justice system. Secondly, the expectation that 'victims' can eventually transcend that identity by translating harm into need, and having those needs met, is incongruous. After all, restorative justice's victim is an identity broadly reinforced by a culture and politics that sustains itself by creating, and governing subjects as, victims. As such, it is often extremely difficult to overcome a victim identity with potentially substantial consequences for entertaining the idea of justice. Restorative governmentalities tie themselves to dominant notions of the victim at the direct cost of recovering a clear alternative to crime-inspired visions of justice.

Restoring victims

It is by now well documented that a core foundation of restorative justice lies in its clearly expressed focus on victims and their 'needs'.[3] As Zehr phrases it, 'The needs of victims for information, validation, vindication, restitution, testimony, safety, and support are the starting points of justice' (2002: 67). This emphasis on victims is a crucial means of distinguishing restorative and criminal justice. Whereas courtroom procedure is framed around determining the guilt of offenders, with little role for victims, restorative justice frames its processes around the needs of the victim.[4] Indeed, as Hoyle notes, 'Restorative justice holds the promise of restoring victims' material and emotional loss, safety, damaged relationships, dignity and self respect' (2002: 101).

Proponents of restorative justice do acknowledge that criminal justice agencies are increasingly reforming themselves to accommodate victims. Increasingly recognising the subaltern status of victims within adversarial styles of justice, with lawyers and offenders dominating procedures, many criminal justice jurisdictions have over the past 25 years supported various reforms that seek to give victims a more prominent role in the

---

3 See, eg, Miers (2004), Strang (2002) and Hoyle and Young (2002).

4 This formulation may display a degree of collective amnesia, for it should be remembered that a little over a century and a half ago, prosecutions were most often brought before courts by victims. Victims have always been central to accusatory processes, and they continue to play a central role in defining events as criminal.

process of justice. As Strang (2002) notes, these reforms have tended to assume two main forms.[5]

On the one hand, under the auspices of the wider victim movement, there is considerable growth in and financial backing for *victim support* agencies that assist victims in dealing with the effects of a criminal event. These agencies have diverse forms and are incorporated differently into criminal justice processes (Hudson, 2003). However, as the term 'support' implies (and for all the diverse incarnations), the primary function of these agencies is to provide stanchions to help crime victims negotiate criminal justice proceedings. They also offer victims assistance in negotiating the aftermath of criminal circumstances, whether at the level of filling in insurance forms or seeking counselling. On the other hand, there are *victims' rights* groups which seek formal rights for victims; an enthusiastically greeted example here is the right to make 'victim impact' statements that will be taken into account in sentencing (Akester, 2002). Both incarnations of the victim movement have helped to reform criminal justice systems across the globe, forging new relations between crime victims and criminal justice processes.

However, for restorative justice proponents, such reforms do not go far enough. And as Miers observes:

> Restorative justice purports to take this relationship and these changes one step further – to one of victim *participation* in the system (2004: 24; emphasis in the original).

Restorative governmentalities espouse victim participation as one of the defining features of their justice, a still significant mark of differentiation from the official system. Thus:

> Restorative justice offers a very different kind of experience, because it gives victims a role in the justice process, and it holds offenders accountable for repairing, as much as possible, the damage caused by their criminal action (Sharpe, 1998: 1).

Restorative governmentalities are therefore relatively unambiguous on the basic – even constitutive – significance of victim participation, empowerment and restoration. Stated differently: without a wholesale reorientation towards victims, there can be no restorative justice in the sense proffered by most

---

5   Much of this section refers directly to Strang, 2002: Chapter 1, but see also Miers (2004) and Hoyle and Young (2002).

advocates.[6] Restorative justice's emphasis on the victim implies some unique expansions to criminal justice approaches: the offender, though defined at the outset through criminal law, is now defined as a harmer of the victim (and community), rather than the state; the community is deemed to be injured via injury to the victim; and the offender can be re-cast as a victim in some sense.

On the strength of these elaborations, restorative governmentalities declare a specific political logic in relation to victims. When a crime is committed, the offender effectively *creates* a victim by the harm, hurt and damages he or she inflicts. From this vantage point, 'crime is primarily a conflict between individuals resulting in injuries to victims, communities and the offenders themselves; only secondarily is it law breaking' (Van Ness, 1993: 259). The differentiation between restorative and criminal justice appears to be decisive at this level, for the harmed victim of crime – rather than the law – assumes centre-stage. Crime victims are thus conferred a special status in that they are deemed to have suffered at the hands of another through no fault of their own. As such:

> ... the term 'crime victim' formally refers to one who has experienced harm as a result of an offence; it is invariably a term of moral approbation suggesting undeserved suffering (Strang, 2002: 2).

This sacrificial logic pervades the discourse on victims, but the sacrifice in question is less about innocence than about the undeserved harm and needs thereby generated. Such needs form the basic starting point of restorative justice.

Victims' needs

As part of their critique of retributive courtroom procedures, restorative justice advocates focus on the 'concrete damage which crime causes to the victim' (Johnstone, 2002: 64). Locating the victim at the heart of restorative justice processes operates on two levels within the discourse. On the one hand, restorative justice advocates provide general accounts of how to conceptualise the

---

6 Thus, Mika and Zehr note that despite differences between restorative justice programs, all advocates 'work toward the restoration of victims, empowering them and responding to their needs as they see them' (see Zehr, 2002: 40).

harms and needs that victims suffer as a result of a criminal act. On the other hand, restorative governmentalities delineate processes to generate individualised, personalised narratives of harm, suffering and need – and in so doing they 'oblige' and facilitate specific victim identities to generate such narratives. Thus, Acorn (2004) refers to what she calls a 'compulsory compassion' demanded by restorative justice processes. The present section focuses on the former level, whereas the next section explores the latter.

In her analysis of victim literatures, Strang notes that, generally, victims require the following from justice in the aftermath of a crime: the desire for less formal processes that take account of their views and provide more information about their cases; the quest for greater participation; respect; 'restoration' of material losses and harms; and 'emotional restoration' often sought through apology and affirmation (2002: 2–3). In line with this, and as noted in Chapter 2, restorative governmentalities usually distinguish between multiple dimensions of harm, including material (physical) damage, psychological (emotional) trauma and relational disruption.[7] These harms generate corresponding needs in victims that could be calculated at a general level.

Physically, victims may have suffered loss of property, personal injury, and may even have lost a loved one. Their material needs are accordingly diverse. Where it can address such needs, restorative justice might assist in the recovery of losses, or get offenders to make amends as far as possible. So, someone who steals another's property may be required to replace it, or to otherwise compensate for the loss. However, restorative governmentalities are keen not to focus exclusively on material restitution, arguing that the emotional and relational fall-out of a crime is often more significant – it is also crucial that offenders accept responsibility for their actions in ways appropriate to a given offence (Braithwaite, 2002). Although such acceptance is important for other reasons within the restorative justice constellation, it has a key role for the restoration of the victim. Indeed, focusing too much on harm as physical

---

7 Strang (2002) also notes several more specific 'needs' that her research indicates frequently demand restoration in victims. Such needs include recovery of: property, security, emotional well-being, safety, dignity, respect, empowerment, social support, a sense of justice, and so on. Attending to such needs would seem to be a precursor to moving beyond victim identity, to allowing victims to 'recover and heal'.

restitution may significantly impede the more complex restorative justice task at hand: 'to repair [the] psychological and relational damage' produced by crime (Johnstone, 2002: 64).

Victims' psychological experiences of harm are also complex and not always predictable (see Hoyle and Young, 2002). However, Zehr's (1990: 20–25) influential text draws on longstanding victimology literatures to formulate a three-phase model of how victims typically respond to crime (especially victims of violence). The model gives some sense of the governmentalities' images of the psychological dimensions of victim harm and the consequently generated needs. For Zehr, the first phase is usually intense emotional shock in which victims are confused, terrified and often feel quite helpless: the victim's self-identity is rocked, leaving him/her bewildered and exposed. This, he argues, is often followed by a second 'recoil' phase in which the victim replaces the intensity of these emotions with other equally intense and forceful emotions (notably guilt, anger, suspicion, etc). These can produce mood swings and alter the victim's self-image. The recoil phase can also lead to relational problems, and may have a distressing – even devastating – effect on many dimensions of the person's life. The harm of these two phases generates specific and diverse needs in victims,[8] and their ability to reconcile themselves with the event is dependent upon their finding ways of addressing these needs. Thus, many feel an intense need to be compensated by the offender, even if only (or perhaps especially) for symbolic reasons.

In addition, victims often have a need for an answer to the 'why me?' question, or need advice on what to do if they are victimised in future (answers to this question given by the offenders are often, Zehr observes, particularly useful in helping victims). Most victims need to find appropriate venues to express themselves and come to understand why they are feeling the way that they do. They also need to regain a sense of 'personal autonomy' – as discussed in Chapter 2 – and security (Zehr, 1990: 27). For those whose needs are met, Zehr proffers a third phase – the recovery or 'reorganisation' phase. This phase helps victims to recuperate by renegotiating the self-identity foisted on them by the aftermath of the criminal event. They are unlikely to overcome the ordeal completely but, Zehr argues, if their unique

---

8   See also Graef (2001: 28–29).

needs are addressed, the event will not 'dominate' their lives. Conversely, if the needs remain unmet, victims are seldom able to move out of the second, 'recoil', phase, and the crime will haunt their lives in perpetuity.

So, the material and emotional needs of crime victims are shaped by contexts of crime, and appropriate responses to these needs are required to enable victims to move beyond their imposed victimhood. Inadequate responses can profoundly affect victims. Their sense of autonomy and trust of others may be affected; this in turn can affect how they relate to others in the future. As Graef notes:

> The impact of crime – even attempted ones – on vulnerable victims can be enormous. Their security is shattered. Moreover, they often blame themselves for what happened. They also suffer a stigma from being victims, as friends and neighbours often feel awkward and unsure of what to say, and stay away (2001: 27).

The impact on victims' relations with others can thus be profound, and restorative justice views its processes as a way of recognising material, psychological and relational needs of victims in an effort to repair damaged relations.

Obliged to be a victim the restorative way

However influential general accounts of the victim responses and needs have been, restorative governmentalities require the production of individual narratives in specific restorative justice settings. Victims are thus encouraged to enunciate the harms they have suffered from the criminal event, to define their consequent needs and to express how they would like these to be addressed. In turn, restorative processes are conceived as helping victims to grapple with the harm of crime and to work with victims (and other stakeholders) to resolve the negative effects of the events as far as possible. As such, restorative justice forums can be seen as adding to the many contemporary sites which today fashion subjects as victims in the name of empowering victims, giving victims a voice, and so on.

However, it is important to note that despite the seeming hypostatisation or reification of the 'victim', much restorative justice discourse ideally regards the victim identity as transient, to be replaced, through appropriate processes, with a restored, non-victim, sense of self. Thus, in many ways, the very idea of victim empowerment implies in restorative justice discourse 'moving beyond' the victim identity:

> From a restorative perspective, 'victims' and 'offender' should be temporary roles. Justice should move quickly to help victims heal, reach closure, and be restored to the community, no longer primarily identified in terms of the harm they have suffered (Sharpe, 1998: 11).

Thus, what might be called the 'contingent ontology' of victimhood is fleetingly referenced by restorative governmentalities. This is an important point, even if it receives relatively short shrift in the discourse. Victims do not exist *sui generis*, in and of themselves; that is, they do not exist in any absolute abstract sense, but are produced through rituals, rules and techniques of power embedded in such social practices as restorative justice techniques. One is not, in essence, a victim; more contentiously, one becomes a victim by participating in contexts designed to create particular forms of the victim identity. Rock captures the point succinctly in the following statement:

> Becoming a 'victim', in short, is an emergent process of signification like many others, possibly involving the intervention and collaboration of others whose impact and meaning changes from stage to stage, punctuated by benchmarks and transitions, and lacking any fixed end state. As an extreme pole, the existential consequences of being a homicide survivor, for instance, are not at first self-evident, but are built up step by step, over time, prompted by professionals and lay people engaged in the processing of crime and death, and embellished by readings provided by relatives, friends and the occasional fellow survivor (2002: 17).

In other words, victims do not appear uniformly, essentially or absolutely as a result of criminal events. Rather, in restorative justice contexts, the victim identity is held out (albeit as a transient identity to be passed through) to those who have suffered at the hands of another. Like all other identities, this one must be negotiated through the relative vicissitudes of contextually available agencies, resources, peer pressures, social expectations, and so on. There are rules and techniques of power that enable subjects to produce themselves as particular kinds of victims.

So the question is, what are the rules and techniques that oblige and facilitate subjects in becoming victims for restorative justice? Of course, given restorative justice's emphasis on victims articulating their own needs, one might say that the rules are contextually negotiated. However, this is only partially so, for there are several elements of the process that oblige – as a condition of partaking in restorative justice forums – participants to become particular kinds of victims. One might consider various case studies, or practitioner guidelines, to indicate the techniques of governance that are mobilised to shape particular victim identities in context.[9] For present purposes, however, let us turn to Umbreit's (2001) discussion of victim-offender mediation (VOM) because it is clear, forthright, succinct and explicitly committed to the broad 'principles' of restorative justice. He defines VOM as a more or less restorative process that allows crime victims to meet offenders 'with the goal of holding the offenders directly accountable while providing important assistance and compensation to victims' (2001: xxxviii). Within this scheme, he argues:

> People who have been victimized by crime have been able to play an active role in the justice process, receive direct information about the crime, express their concerns about the full impact of the criminal behaviour on their lives, and negotiate with the offender a mutually acceptable plan for restoring losses to the greatest extent possible (2001: xxxviii).

In his discussion of how to deploy 'victim-sensitive mediation', Umbreit (2001: Chapter 2) offers detailed guidelines for potential mediations. Interpreting his framework on the admitted bias of seeking what it says about victim identities, one gleans how subjects are conceived *as victims*, and how restorative justice forums like VOM seek to shape (oblige) specific victim identities. My exegesis suggests four main areas through which the postulated ideal identity becomes clear in his discussion: case selection; preparing the way to adopting restorative justice's victim identity; shaping the identity through restorative justice processes; and consequences of failing to adopt the victim identity on offer.

Selecting cases

Umbreit makes clear that mediators should consider the 'readiness' of subjects for engagement with restorative justice

---

9   See, eg, Braithwaite (2002), Strang (2002) and Umbreit (2001: 267–90).

procedures, whose success depends in large measure on appropriate selection criteria to determine which parties will likely benefit from the process. The basic criterion must be 'the victim's ability to represent their interests and express their needs' (2001: 26). This is the kernel of what it is to be a victim in restorative justice terms: a subject who has clear interests and needs brought into sharp relief by a criminal event.

Moreover, an ideal victim is one who not only has the capacity to know what these are, but is able to 'represent' them. The recursive nature of latter concept is instructive, for it embeds the idea that needs and interests are necessarily 'present', and the effective victim can make them 'present' (re-present) through language, story telling and the like. Only those subjects capable of delivering on what is presumed to be the basis of victimhood are considered appropriate cases for restorative justice. This is a requirement for victims who will *actively* participate in the process (Hoyle, 2002: 102).

Preparing selected subjects to become victims

Reading through Umbreit's handbook and guidelines for effective restorative justice processes, I am struck by the emphasis placed on preparing victims (and offenders) for the mediation: 'The importance of preparing participants for mediation or dialogue cannot be overstated. This is the most time-consuming part of the work of the mediator' (2001: 275). What is significant about this emphasis is its internal tension: if victims are the necessary product of a criminal event, and restorative justice takes these as its starting point, then why would preparation be so significant? Strang provides a self-referential response in which the identity of being a restorative justice victim can be placed in jeopardy without proper preparation:

> *Insufficient preparation of victims* (and of offenders) regarding their role in the conferences, their expectations about the outcome, and their rights in terms of requesting reparation can have serious negative consequences for victims (Strang, 2002: 150; emphasis in the original).

'Preparing' is thus an important point at which subjects are socialised into the basic tenets of restorative justice's victim identity.[10] They are geared to align their expectations so as not to anticipate too much and be ready to meet offenders, and they are made aware that their participation is always voluntary. Umbreit notes the importance of mediators meeting with victims in advance of mediation sessions, if possible at their homes (to place them in familiar territory). Here, the initial contact is meant to 'establish credibility and rapport' (2001: 29). This allows the mediator to go over the main features of VOM and to develop some sense of the victim's view. In general, it allows him or her 'to prepare victims for what lies ahead' (2001: 29).

The mediator is also advised to use the pre-mediation conference to help subjects: 'Victims may appreciate assistance in identifying losses experienced in the crime and present needs related to the crime' (Umbreit, 2001: 31). At the same time, the mediator could help them to think about 'what it would take to repair the harm done' (2001: 31). That is, part of socialising subjects into a restorative justice victim role is encouraging them to adopt an identity that focuses on losses (material, emotional and relational), needs and resolutions to these. Victim support information may then also be supplied, to cement the preparation for what it is to be a victim the restorative way.

Shaping victims through mediation

The socialisation of a restorative victim identity continues at the mediation session itself, where the mediator will have spent some time carefully arranging the physical space for the session[11]

---

10 Towards the end of his comprehensive synopsis, Umbreit focuses on three extreme VOM case studies, involving parents of murdered victims who meet with the imprisoned murderers. The parents are made aware of (by victim services in two cases) and discuss the process with mediators (viewing videos of the process is often the first exposure). The parents are reluctant to participate in the process and are especially concerned about confronting the offender (see Hoyle, 2002: 105; Strang, 2002). However, they agree to do so after careful preparation (eg, they are shown videos of other victim-offender mediations); the VOM seems to play to parents' completely understandable desire for more information about their child's premature death, and makes offenders aware of the devastating effects of their murderous actions.

11 Interestingly, some advocates do not see the need for victims to be present in restorative justice process – they can still be active in resolving their disputes. As Hoyle puts it, 'victim participation' should not *require* their attendance at a meeting with the offender. Choosing not to participate in the session should not rule out 'indirect mediation' (2002: 105–06).

in order to create a 'relaxed, positive atmosphere' (Umbreit, 2001: 20). He or she will begin the session by outlining the ground-rules of the process (eg, respectful talk, etc) and make clear to everyone that participation is voluntary. The mediator must use 'victim-sensitive' language at all times (eg, avoiding a term like 'forgive' in case it places pressure on someone who does not want to do so). The victim usually is asked to begin the process by narrating him/herself in relation to the crime. In voicing that story, the victim is encouraged to be respectful of, and talk directly to, the offender. Part of that story, eventually, should include a statement of 'what it would take for them to feel that things have been resolved' (2001: 54).

Moreover, 'If the parties are finding it difficult to come up with resolution options, mediators may want to remind them of possibilities discussed during the premediation interview' (2001: 54). The victim should be encouraged to make reasonable demands, and should not be allowed 'to recover more than the amount of the actual loss' (2001: 55). If there are confrontations or the dialogue gets too 'heated', the mediator should reframe positions in less charged language, and try to move the discussion forward: 'Neutral rephrasing of facts and issues helps remove value-laden language and balance intense emotions' (2001: 61). My point in highlighting these blueprints is to illustrate, if only in sketchy outline, the sort of techniques used to help shape the identity of restorative justice's victim. No doubt, there are differences between sessions, and indeed between types of restorative justice forums, but all embrace equivalents of a secular confessional in which the victim is required – as a condition of participating in the process – to adopt a delimited identity designed to help bring about restoration.

Refusal and consequence

Certain actions are taken as effective refusals to accept the ground-rules of mediation. Examples would include disrespectful attacks on the offender's character, abusive emotional tirades, unreasonable requests for recompense, physical outbursts, and so on. In such cases, the advice to the mediator is clear: end the mediation session on the strength that the ground-rules have been broken and any semblance of restoration is unlikely. This guideline, though relatively uncomplicated, requires a degree of judgment on the part of the mediator – it also indicates the outer limits of what is acceptable behaviour for anyone who is to adopt the identity of 'victim' in the context of restorative justice (see Acorn, 2004).

In sum, the VOM guidelines implicitly (or explicitly) oblige a victim to adopt a particular identity structured around the following fundamentals. A restorative victim is an individual subject who is able to identify his or her interests and needs in relation to a criminal event. This subject is encouraged to have reasonable expectations of restorative justice processes, and recognise him/herself as a voluntary as well as active participant therein. The victim is expected to respect the mediator (restorative justice referee) as a kind of counsellor who can help to identify interests, losses and needs that emerge as a result of a criminal event. The ideal victim here becomes an active, positive participant in determining how to find a resolution to the experience. This identity must have the ability – with the active help of restorative justice agents – to re-present needs generated by crime at conference/mediation, and have a good idea of what would repair the harm done.

Restoration to regular community life is the goal and this may require meeting with offenders and other community members. In any such meetings, victims are encouraged to express themselves clearly, but should always abide by the ground-rules of the process (otherwise it will be terminated). This requires being respectful but honest, such that the subject must narrate a plausible (and publicly presented) truth about him/herself in relation to the criminal event. In this representation, the victim should communicate directly with the offender, listen to others and allow mediators to reframe blunt formulations. They should keep control of their emotions as far as possible, and never become abusive or revengeful. The victim should be reasonable about losses, and remain open-minded (brainstorming) when trying to work towards an effective resolution. If possible, victims are encouraged to forgive, but should not feel obligated to do so. As such, we have at least a sense of the 'ideal type' of victim identity that restorative justice processes are designed to restore and reconcile with a broader community.

The *imitor* paradox, victims and consequences

We have seen how restorative justice governmentalities claim to be distinct from adversarial justice processes as they require the active participation and empowerment of victims in resolving their own conflicts. Victims are not, so the reasoning goes, sidelined as passive witnesses to adversarial theatres of justice. In this way, victim participation is an important way of distinguishing the two approaches to justice. Even if, as noted, victims are increasingly evident in criminal justice systems through victim support services and are given particular rights in judicial procedure, restorative justice requires a far more active participation of victims in all phases of its processes. Victims are to take hold of their predicaments and assume responsibility for defining needs created by a crime as well as communicate how these can be met.

Without denying any differences, it is important to note that both criminal and restorative calculations of justice proceed on a common assumption that victim identities exist because of the harms rendered by criminal offenders. That is, neither calculation of justice is possible without the prior conceptualisation of the category 'victim' as created by crime. Both calculations share grounding concepts and are predicated upon a common assumption that 'victims' (and offenders) always exist as definable identities as soon as a crime is committed. Notwithstanding the important question of whether or not the idea of a victim is ontologically secure, the assumption that the victim – however defined – constitutes a starting point for both conceptions of justice militates against the claim that empowering victims is a rudimentary difference between restorative and criminal justice.

To make the point another way, one could argue that a veritable difference would be present if one were to posit notions of justice beyond any *a priori* allegiance to the victim identity. To be sure, it may be difficult to erase notions of victimhood when the suffering involved is great; but many events involve degrees of anguish that may call for remedies other than the application of victim *personae*. Indeed, for some cases that filter into both criminal and restorative justice systems, the designation of victim may not be sought by affected parties, or indeed may not be appropriate to the situation. One might even argue that alternative calculations of justice are likely to achieve maximum subject participation precisely in those cases where suffering is not so great as to demand the designation of the victim and the application of law (eg, in homicide or violent assault cases, etc). In cases of petty theft, for example, it may be difficult to designate victim identities – as with the classical example of a poverty-stricken parent pilfering bread from a corporate superstore to feed his children. The parent may be as much –

perhaps even more – a 'victim' of systemic inequality than the superstore may be a victim of the theft.

The point to make is this: it may be timely and appropriate for self-proclaimed 'alternatives' to attempt formulations of justice without imitating some of the key criminal justice assumptions. The greatest contributions of a proclaimed alternative might well be to accept its limitations and, within designated domains of operation, predicate itself on different assumptive foundations from the approach it claims to arrogate. Without so doing, the governmentality leads itself into further paradoxical terrains, two of which are directly related to problems attendant upon obliging subjects to be victims.

Empowerment as a victim?

Even a casual observer is likely to be struck by the paradoxical claim that restorative justice seeks to empower victims as victims. The question that immediately surfaces here is this: what sort of empowerment is ever available to victims *as* victims? What sort of alternative is a justice that depends fundamentally on the perpetual flow of victims? The etymology of the term brings this implicit critique into finer focus. The term 'victim' 'originally denoted a "person or animal killed as sacrifice"; the more general notion of "someone who suffers from or is killed by something" is a secondary development' (Ayto, 1990: 558). Victims suffer, and suffering is a condition of being defined a 'victim'.

This etymology alerts us to the notion that the crime victim is by definition someone who has been disempowered in some way, who has involuntarily sacrificed security, autonomy, material possessions, self-preservation and the like. Most surviving victims seek to transcend the circumstances that lead to the disempowered identity, and this raises a particular question: what purpose lies behind attempts to empower subjects through an identity that is, by definition, disempowered? Is it not more appropriate to try to escape that identity, perhaps by 'empowering' subjects through another identity? Might it not make more sense to support those who have suffered in pursuing identities that are not, by definition, disempowered?

Such questions allude to the problem of obliging those who have suffered at the hands of others to assume a disempowered, sacrificial victim role as a condition of alleviating their suffering. It may even constitute a double victimisation that does little or nothing to enable subjects to engage politically with, and so substantially alter, the broader social conditions that have generated their suffering to begin with. There is therefore a tragic incongruity involved in promoting a justice that empowers victims *as* victims, and which depends essentially on the continued presence of victims. The stance is particularly pernicious when one considers that this identity is itself predicated – by definition – upon the continued presence of suffering. If the objective of justice is to rectify or move beyond the situation of victimhood, then is it not appropriate that justice measures should seek different auspices for engaging a victimising event? For political engagement with this event to be effective (empowered), the involvement of political identities beyond that of individual victimhood may indeed be crucial. No doubt, different political identities could surface as a result of suffering – but they cannot be beleaguered by it without ensconcing themselves in the very suffering they seek to remedy. It may be helpful to refer to the diverse identities assumed by grassroots activists, social reformers, issue campaigners, etc, and the effective political engagements that they sometimes inspire. Engaging such a politics does not require subjects to define themselves through restorative justice's images of what an empowered victim entails.

Stated differently, experiences of injustice and suffering may well frame aspirations to justice, but they could also serve as a basis for changing the social conditions that lead to particular forms of victimisation in the first place. If one insists on speaking the language of empowerment, its vocabulary might centre on effective engagements with political forces that have generated a particular situation. The point is to transform – rather than cling onto – unwanted products (for example, the victim) of the very social conditions that generate particular situations in the first place. Restorative justice's focus on empowering victims may certainly redress the criminal justice system's failure to acknowledge key phenomenological experiences of what it is to suffer at the hands of another. However, its emphasis on the politics of victimhood would seem to entrench, more than deliver, people from the founding auspices of the criminal justice system.

Transcending victimhood – by becoming a victim?

Moving beyond the 'temporary' identity of 'victim' is a basic and logical goal of *restorative* governmentalities. Victims are assigned the role of actively participating in refashioning their identity in the service of that end. Afterwards, as noted above, restorative justice is predicated upon, and is sustained on the basis of there being, victims who participate in curative processes. In other words, this governmentality wants to have its figurative cake and eat it too. By definition, it demands that people identify as victims, only then to insist that through this identification they release themselves from the identity. The recursive logic is as paradoxical as it is contorted: identify as an actively participating victim, for this will lead you eventually to overthrow the self-same identity.

Transcending victimhood is in many cases a laudable quest, offering subjects a different way of dealing with injustice and suffering. It also implies the aspiration to new ways of being, beyond the conditions that have generated victims in the first place. However, it is difficult to imagine how such a quest, or aspiration, could effectively be realised by affirming the identity of individual victims – the very identity one seeks to overcome. So long as a conception of justice is predicated on serving individual victims, the stage is set for securing the ongoing supply of victim identities. Indeed, without victims to be restored, the whole logic of restorative justice, and its quest to empower 'victims', becomes impossible. The dissolution of victim identities through restoration appears then to be predicated upon a never-ending supply of victims.

If this suggests an implication of the *imitor* paradox, it also raises questions about dealing with broad relational injustices by attempting to restore individual victims. If expunging injustice is key to the quest for justice, remedial measures should correspond to the scale and form of the power relations at hand. Consider, for example, sexual harassment cases. Although locally experienced, few would contest that specific incidents of sexual harassment are spawned by the interaction of wider power (patriarchal) relations and broadly produced cultures of sexuality. Yet dealing with each case on an individual basis, viewing the matter as amenable to, or even demanding, *individual* resolution is to address but one dimension of something far broader and more complex. To be sure, specific subjects who suffer from such harassment should receive assistance, but if the aim is to pursue a just condition where such injustices are expunged, then the broad socio-political relations that nurture such events may need to be engaged directly.

Changing the conditions that generate subjects who are so victimised requires a concerted political effort directed at numerous facets of the relations at hand – cultural, social and political. The latter involves much more than restoring each individual case to a semblance of consensual communal well-being. After all, conflict often brings the dangers of such communal being to the fore, and restorative justice loses an opportunity to engage broader power strategies if it simply focuses on restoring individual victims. Arrogating generalised effects of local power relations (inequality), as if they were capable of resolution on a case-by-case basis, misunderstands their political breadth and complexity. Tragically, affirming individual victims may even help to perpetuate the underlying power relations by dispersing tensions and deflecting attention away from their general exercise.

Just implications

Thus, here too, in the realm of the victim, the *imitor* paradox and its attendant tension is replicated. By placing their governmental eggs in the victim basket, advocates of restorative justice unnecessarily limit the degree to which they can offer visions and practices of justice not already pre-dependent on a key hosting auspice of the (criminal justice) calculations that they seek to transcend. This may have some advantages in political contexts that privilege the voices of victim identities, but it has serious negative implications for any long-term attempt to think seriously about the promise of justice in new terms.

For example, defining empowerment as involving individual victims taking control of the aftermath of 'crime' has the effect of not seeking other ways of engaging the underlying power relations that have generated undesired circumstances in the first place. First and foremost, empowerment must surely involve a way of effectively engaging and transforming unjust conditions so as to prevent future occurrences. Those who have suffered through a particular set of circumstances may be encouraged to seek politically engaged identities that work to achieve social and cultural transformations. The promise of justice is precisely about thinking how to be with others in social relations that work against the replication of undesired, unjust circumstances. By encouraging subjects to take control of the aftermath of criminal events as victims, restorative justice turns its back on the possibility of thinking about justice as inspiring new forms of life in which unjust interactions are collectively expunged. What is at stake here is much more than a restoration, or even reformation, of a presumed community; instead, justice may well be a way of contemplating collective solidarity without relying on concepts – like victim, offender and community – that are already implicated in fabricating the social conditions at hand.

Similarly, by emphasising the role of victims, advocates of restorative justice often individualise collective injustices and confuse the restoration of individuals with the more difficult quest of expunging broader relations of injustice. Perhaps this task is more properly considered in relation to the role of community restoration, and, as we shall see in Chapter 5, restorative justice seeks to restore communities as well as individuals. It may even restore, some will argue, communities precisely through restoring individual victims and offenders. However, the point here is a different one. Through the very practices of restorative justice – conferences, mediation – procedures are directed towards particular individuals as the sources of and solutions to a specific criminal event. In effect, this individualises justice and disables subjects from engaging power relations as political agents beyond individual victims, offenders and so-called affected members of a presumed community. There is no attempt, for example, to approach given sets of circumstances as arising from collective political relations (for example, patriarchal relations, economic disadvantages, etc), or from generalised relational inequities. Nor is there an attempt to understand particular cases as examples of far broader trends within a given relational complex. The possibility that specific cases may be representative of more general relational tendencies is effectively displaced by the attempt to restore individuals to healthy orders (see Chapter 2, above). Yet if given social and political relations keep producing unjust circumstances, then one wonders how individualising specific cases and agents, seeking individual resolutions to complex relational injustices, is likely to bring about collective transformations. In so doing, the general roots of injustice are completely overlooked. Restoring victims to a status quo may secure an ongoing flow of victims but does not directly engage broader relational matrices that breed the injustices to which restorative justice responds.

Finally, predicating restorative visions of justice on basic criminal justice concepts (such as, notably, the victim) narrows calculations of justice to the auspices of dominant visions. This diametrically opposes the experimental, open thinking about justice that launched restorative justice in the first place. The attempt to formulate an alternative to criminal justice visions and approaches to crime is undercut significantly by the continued acceptance of several key assumptions. Worse still, restorative justice reinforces visions of criminal justice as fundamental, essential and thereby replicates its very auspices.

An important upshot of the present chapter is this: one might begin to ask whether or not it is possible to envisage justice without some of these basic criminal justice precepts. Might we envisage justice without notions of victim, or even perhaps crime? We shall return to such matters, but for now it is enough to problematise this unqualified quest for victim empowerment and individual restoration as the critical objective of alternative conceptions of justice. This is especially important in a political ethos that has come, for the reasons speculated upon at the outset of this chapter, to elevate individual victim identities, but which is less focused on alleviating injustice and suffering in more general ways.

The growing attachment to critical rationalities of the 18th century, commonly evoked through abbreviated conceptions such as 'the Enlightenment', left unmistakable imprints on virtually all spheres of everyday life. In matters of ethics, as of transport, government, statecraft, architecture, art, music, law, public sanitation, and so on, enlightened reason extended its reign to far-flung global reaches – 'awakening', to paraphrase Kant on his reading of Hume, humanity from its 'dogmatic slumbers'. The rise of classical jurisprudence was one of its decisive yields. Through the writings of such philosophers as Voltaire, Montesquieu, Bentham and Beccaria, Enlightenment legal thinking aspired to justice, equality and fairness, and freedom from undue political influence, arbitrary process, excessive punishments and corruption. Such, at any rate, is the story – and the model.

Several of the principles developed and adopted by such protagonists were directed specifically to how offenders, or alleged offenders, should be perceived and treated. For example, the rights of the accused should be protected and upheld, from the moment of accusation throughout their contact with the criminal justice system. Laws must codify clearly and precisely the sorts of acts sanctioned or prohibited, documenting rationally calibrated punishments to correspond directly with the severity of a given infringement. Punishment is not to be excessive, and is to be invoked only when offenders have transgressed criminal laws representing an implicit social order, thereby violating other people's rights or somehow wounding an abstracted public body.

Briefly put – for it is familiar – the 'classical' reasoning behind punishing offenders was as follows. Individual offenders, as rational and free beings, freely choose to break a law for their own purposes or gain (pleasure). They thereby transgress a social order. Appropriate levels of punishment should inflict pain upon an offender proportional to (and not in excess of) the severity of the offence. Since the purpose of punishment is to deter the commission of future crimes both by the offender and within the general population, punishments must be 'swift and certain' to ensure that subjects come to associate offending acts with corresponding punishments.

This rationale for dealing with offenders has for centuries thrived, developed and been sustained through various legal reforms. It continues to justify consequential bits of contemporary criminal justice institutions. However, as is well documented,[1] this vision of offending was challenged by traces of another – eugenically- and scientifically-based – approach which claimed an ability to decipher the natural causes of crime. The so-called 'criminal anthropology' of the late 19th century, popularised by Cesare Lombroso, referred to social evolutionism when producing an image of criminal offenders as 'atavistic' throwbacks to more primitive stages of human evolution. His work posited the idea that some people are 'born criminal', the *homo criminalis*; they do not rationally choose to offend but rather inherit a natural make-up that predisposes them to offend. From this vantage, the appropriate response to criminal behaviour is thus not to punish but to manage, not so much to inflict pain as to identify, classify and predict criminality. The quest to predict criminality from genes, to rehabilitate through treatment, or to develop other empirically-orientated approaches to offenders fall decidedly within the sphere of criminal anthropology's basic maxims.

Although other images of offenders (for example, as social actors) continue to abound within criminal justice discourses, erstwhile classical and positivist visions of offenders remain profoundly influential, enabling the relational complexes that comprise the contemporary courts and prisons. Situating itself against these traditions' values, conceptions and processes, restorative justice claims to provide radically different images of the offender. Embracing key tenets of the governmentality, Zehr notes that:

> The criminal justice system is concerned about holding offenders accountable, but that means making sure offenders get the punishments they deserve. Little in the process encourages offenders to understand the consequences of their actions or to empathize with victims (2002: 16).

---

1 See, eg, Valier (2002).

Furthermore, he argues that the 'adversarial game' actively encourages offenders to adopt defensive postures to look out for their own interests. As a result, offenders are not required to confront the limitations of their own reasoning, or the effects of their harmful offending on victims (Graef, 2001). Their responsibility is abstracted to legal requirement, and this discourages them from being empathic towards those they have harmed (Sharpe, 1998). In addition, the retributive punishment inflicted encourages recidivism not least because its alienating and demeaning structures encourage low self-esteem; it also does not require offenders to face up to the consequences of their actions, or to take responsibility for cleaning up the material, psychological and relational messes their offences often yield. Moreover, they are not required to face the 'needs' that led them to offend, or the 'needs' such offending behaviour produces within (Braithwaite, 2002; Sharpe, 1998). Restorative justice is expressly designed, then, to hold offenders properly accountable to victims and communities for the offences (serving custodial time does not necessarily satisfy that requirement), to encourage 'personal transformation', and to help with their reintegration into the community.

This critique of criminal justice provides key points of departure for the altered paradigm through which restorative governmentalities approach offenders. It is also one way of reinforcing the claim that restorative and (classically inspired, positivist, etc) criminal justice approaches are distinct. Yet even with these brief statements in mind, one might raise questions about the sort of difference possible between restorative paradigms and criminal jurisprudence when the former relies so fundamentally on the latter's notions of the 'individual offender' as someone who has committed a crime. The present chapter directs itself to precisely this issue, by exploring influential images of the 'offender' within restorative governmentalities, before turning to the prevailing omniscience of the *imitor* paradox in context.

Restorative justice's offender

As we have noted, the offender is deemed an important participant in restorative justice processes and programs. Even if it emphasises victim-centred practices, restorative justice's quest to restore right relations when a crime is committed demands the involvement of those who are responsible for criminal acts. It is they who must be held accountable, make amends for the hurt they generate, work on themselves to bring about identity changes, and make progress towards reintegration into given communities. If this underscores the critical role that offenders play in restorative governmentalities, it also suggests the importance of understanding how such identities are approached in context.

The word 'offender' has an interesting etymological lineage. It derives from the Latin word *offendere*, which is made up of the parts *'of'*, meaning 'against', and *'fendere'*, 'to strike'. Combining these parts we have 'to strike against', which implies that there is something struck and a subject which does the striking. Since at least the 14th century, the concept of offender has been attached to various meaning frameworks. However, within Enlightenment criminal legal developments of the 18th and 19th centuries, 'offender' was given a specific meaning: 'someone who commits a crime'.[2] Restorative justice governmentalities do not contest the modern meaning horizons within which the offender now stands; rather, they add to its vistas and conjure the *dramatis persona* of the offender in somewhat unique ways.

To begin with, restorative governmentalities take for granted that an offender commits a crime. Procedurally, most restorative justice programs require offenders to admit to committing a crime before being allowed to participate in their processes. However, unlike criminal justice approaches, restorative justice processes seek to define crime not as a transgression against criminal law that precipitates courtroom dramas designed to determine whether, and which precise, criminal statutes are transgressed. Rather, as Zehr argues, 'crime is a violation of people and relationships' (2002: 21);[3] it happens to 'real people' and generates – as noted – harm and needs (Sharpe, 1998). And so, instead of focusing on 'just deserts' for guilty offenders, restorative justice attends to the harms and 'obligations' that crime creates. It focuses especially on what offenders can do to 'put things right' with victims and communities.

In context, then, the offender is not classicism's 'free, rational agent', or criminal anthropology's *homo criminalis*; rather he or she is the generator of contextual harms, the bearer of needs and obligations and the one who is to make amends for causing those harms. As Zehr puts it:

---

2 See www.allwords.com/word-offender.html.
3 See also Zehr (1990: 181).

By his actions, our offender has violated another person. He has also violated relationships of trust within the community (1990: 44).

And it is these violations that must be confronted. The offender, as one who strikes against, must now take responsibility for working with those who are harmed to repair and remove – as far as possible – the damage done. Zehr continues:

When someone wrongs another, he or she has an obligation to make things right. This is what justice should be about (1990: 197).

Restorative justice's image of the accountable offender who is required to face unique obligations of his or her making inspires techniques designed to educate offenders about various dimensions of their criminal behaviour. Through such techniques:

Offenders become aware that crime is committed, not against an abstraction, but against someone real – a person like themselves – and also against their community, which is affected by what happened (Graef, 2001: 18).

As such, restorative justice tries to bring home to offenders the sorts of responsibilities they must assume for committing a crime. It is thus concerned with making clear *'offender responsibility for repairing harm'* (Zehr, 2002: 21 – emphasis in the original). As with victims, we encounter the governmentalities' focus on harm; with specific reference to the offender, however, concepts of harm are evoked in unique ways and for specific discursive purposes.

Offender accountability, identity reform and communal reintegration

Even though victims emerge as the primary focus of restorative justice's attempts to deal with the harms generated by criminal action, offenders are viewed as the prime causes of harm. As such, they are most responsible for repairing the damages of their offending behaviour. Consequently, restorative processes are designed to provide venues that require offenders to recognise, confront and be held accountable for the effects of their criminal actions on both victims and wider communities:

The goals of restorative justice regarding offenders seem straightforward: to get offenders to accept responsibility for their actions and to make amends and to reintegrate (or sometimes integrate for the first time) such offenders into the community of law-abiding citizens (Johnstone, 2002: 95).

The basic assumption here is that criminal hurt and damage not only affect victims and communities, but also generate specific obligations and needs in offenders. At root, the encompassing obligation is for the harm generator to make appropriate and meaningful amends. It is noted too that restorative practices are not usually a 'soft option' for offenders (Johnstone, 2002). On the contrary, restorative governmentalities point out that it is often much more difficult for offenders to face victims and/or their families than to sit passively in court and face the abstracted admonishments of courtroom procedures (Braithwaite, 2002). The latter provide ways for offenders to evade accountability and responsibility, but the former demand that they confront the people their actions have hurt.

Offenders are also said to be affected by their crimes, and experience needs which justice ought to address if it aims to avoid future recidivism. They often feel profound remorse for their behaviour and so experience a need to be held accountable and to make things right (Sharpe, 1998). In addition, many experience a need to be reintegrated into the community (see Zehr, 2002: 17; 1990: 40ff). But restorative justice does not allow them to address any of these needs without fully confronting the harm that they have produced. Added to this, so the reasoning goes, offenders are held accountable in ways that go far beyond the criminal justice system's narrow emphasis on punishment: they must listen to the hurt they have inflicted upon others, and be made to understand the tangible consequences of their offending behaviour. *Post hoc* rationalisations and justifications of the event, stereotypical reifications about victims, or other attempts to escape taking responsibility for what they have done must be challenged by restorative processes. Furthermore, their behaviour creates an obligation to right wrongs. Once they accept responsibility for their violations, offenders 'must be allowed and encouraged to help what will happen to make things right, then take steps to repair the damage' (Zehr, 1990: 42).

Since victim harms are construed as material, psychological or relational, making amends may involve material restitution, corrective rituals, community service, explanations to victims, apologies and other ways of addressing the needs of victims and communities. Zehr conveys the overall tenets of the approach by stating that 'society' implicitly addresses the offender thus:

You have done wrong by violating someone. You have an obligation to make the wrong right. You may choose to do so willingly, and we will allow you to be involved in figuring out how this should be done. If you do not choose to accept this responsibility, however, we will have to decide for you what needs to be done and will require you to do it (1990: 198).

In parenthesis, the reason for involving offenders in the process of deciding how to restore right relations is probably not unrelated to Bentham's call for 'indirect governance' noted in Chapter 1. To recall, he outlined the potential yield of shaping a subject's motivations and will as a way of preventing (as opposed to merely responding to) unwanted actions. Empowered participation may provide a lasting shift in offender identity since it is *indirectly* engendered as opposed to *directly* coerced.[4] Regardless, restorative justice's aim is to help transform offenders from harm-generating to harm-reducing identities. It nurtures personal identity changes designed to change personalities otherwise hell-bent on violating and hurting others. The potential link with harm reduction strategies in other areas of criminology and criminal justice is implied but not developed in restorative governmentalities.

Although restorative governmentalities focus on offenders as harm-producers, they thus also emphasise the importance of encouraging identity changes within given people. If the overall sum of future crimes committed is to be reduced, one needs to decrease the number of criminal identities who perpetrate the crimes in the first place. As such, restorative justice seeks to ensure that an offender's identity is a transitory one; one that can be discarded as he or she moves towards reintegration within a given community. Supporters recognise that if they are to offer a successful strategy, they must provide opportunities for the personal development of offenders, and ease their return to the community. Offender stigmatisation is seen as particularly detrimental to successful reintegration (Braithwaite, 2002; Zehr, 2002).

With such matters in mind, restorative governmentalities isolate at least two further visions of need and harm as applied to offenders. First, several restorative justice advocates acknowledge that an offender's past life generates the need to

---

4 I have elsewhere described the subtle ways in which power operates in community mediation contexts, and the general precepts could be translated to other restorative contexts (see Pavlich, 1996b).

commit crime, and this past is to be confronted and set right. Though not proffered as an excuse for overlooking transgression, Braithwaite's concept of positive shaming recognises that offenders are sometimes poorly socialised and lack the necessary social and cultural literacy skills to integrate effectively into a community (Braithwaite, 2002: 98). This sometimes leads to criminal action but, through relatively simple corrections, lives of crime can be arrested. Braithwaite's (1989) idea of 'reintegrative shaming' (as opposed to other more destructive forms of shaming) provides a foundation for restorative techniques which seek to alter offender identity in this way. He sums up the tenets of the theory thus:

> The core claims are (1) that tolerance of crime makes things worse; (2) that stigmatization, or disrespectful, outcasting shaming of crime, makes crime worse still; and (3) that reintegrative shaming, or disapproval of the act within a continuum of respect for the offender and terminated by rituals of forgiveness, prevents crime (2002: 74).

So, the reintegration of offenders requires a positive form of shaming in which offending identities are transformed, thus enabling them to assume productive roles within existing communities. Offenders must be given opportunities to (re)join communal formations once they fully appreciate, as well as take responsibility for, make amends for and apologise sincerely for their harmful criminal action. This also means providing them with life skills (anger management, drug and alcohol programs, literacy programs, etc) to achieve the necessary changes that will help them move from offender to law-abiding citizen (Sharpe, 1998).

Secondly, some advocates argue that offenders should themselves be seen as harmed by the act of committing a crime (Zehr, 1990: 200). This political rationale derives in part from the view that because of their intrinsically social nature, human beings are themselves harmed when they violate other human beings or trust relations (Consedine, 1995). Just as victims harmed by criminal acts have needs, so the self-harmed offender experiences needs that adversarial, abstracted criminal justice systems simply ignore. By contrast, restorative justice processes are designed to recognise and deal with such needs by enabling offenders to understand their responsibilities as well as providing avenues that allow them to make things right.

From this vantage point, then, if offenders are to be reformed – restored rather than simply punished or rehabilitated – they should be required to understand the consequences of their actions, and approach future actions with those understandings clearly in mind. As Graef puts it, restorative justice (and specifically mediation) encourages offenders to 'own the responsibility for their crime' and once aware of the effects of their action should 'reassess their future behaviour in light of this knowledge' (2001: 33). Thus, the views of victims and community should be expressed unequivocally, and offenders given a chance to respond. Zehr[5] again usefully sums up the political rationale:

> Offenders have many needs ... They need to have their stereotypes and rationalizations – their 'misattributions' – about the victim and the event challenged. They may need to learn to be more responsible. They may need to develop employment and interpersonal skills ... to channel anger and frustration in more appropriate ways ... to develop a positive and healthy self-image ... Like victims, unless such needs are met, closure is impossible (1990: 200).

In addition, the offender is seen as a key actor in helping to meet the victim's need, and in redressing the harm that he or she has caused.

From this sketch, one is able to discern the identity of restorative justice's offender as someone who: may in the past have been harmed and often needs coping/social skills; has committed a crime that violates and hurts others; is harmed by the criminal act which creates the need to understand, confront and take responsibility for that harm; must help to define ways to make amends and restore right relations (involving perhaps reintegrative shaming); and should by way of closure be reintegrated into an existing community.

For all the attention directed to offenders, it is important to restate that the governmentality regards their needs as distinctly subordinate to those of victims – the focal point of its practices. As Johnstone puts it, while restorative justice is:

> ... concerned with the healing of offenders, this goal is to be pursued only insofar as it can be made compatible with the goal of achieving justice for their victims. Offenders must be held accountable to victims for the harm they have caused and must

---

5 See also Sharpe (1998: 9).

make serious efforts to repair such harm before they can expect *their* needs to be attended to. However ... by holding offenders accountable and encouraging them to make amends for their behaviour we are already beginning to meet their needs (2002: 95).

Even with this caveat firmly in mind, however, it is clear that by claiming to deal with offenders in unique ways, restorative governmentalities distinguish their approaches from criminal justice arenas.

The *imitor* paradox and the offender

Despite using its visions of offender as a marker of uniqueness, restorative governmentalities again face the problem of maintaining difference by relying on a concept that comprises a foundation of criminal justice frameworks. The claim to approach offenders in a radically different way is predicated upon the assumption of 'criminal' offenders existing in the first place. Of course, here one encounters contextual reverberations of the *imitor* paradox, which traces this area of the governmentality in three rather specific ways.

First, the governmentality predicates images of offender harm on prior conceptions of *crime* as a legally defined entity. Secondly, envisaging the offender necessarily as an *individual* perpetrator of 'crime' locks one into a political logic that holds individuals responsible for the harms surrounding 'criminal' events. Here, since the criminal entity is most often pictured as an individual, it is individuals who are held to account by making necessary amends. Though there may be differences in understanding, restorative governmentalities replicate a criminal justice emphasis on individual (as opposed to, say, systemic) responsibility. The politics of restorative justice is thus by and large centred on offender reform, as opposed to a wider politics of social resistance and change. The offender, rather than, say, broader power relations, is always the one who is to make amends – an approach that is also well developed in criminal justice institutions.

Thirdly, the governmentality replicates the criminal justice view that criminal harm is largely an offender's responsibility. That is, the offender is the generator of harms that require amelioration. If this shared assumption deflects attention away from the possibility that criminal law may itself in several instances be a harm-creator, it also shows how both visions of justice derive from a common emphasis on offender as harm-creator. It is perhaps worth dwelling further on each of these three replications of the *imitor* paradox, for they provide important openings with which to imagine alternative formulations of justice.

Crime and the offender

One question that surfaces when considering the concept of an offender who 'strikes against' is brief: 'Against what?' Criminal justice traditions have canvassed that question repeatedly through jurisprudence and political theory centred on state sovereignty, legal reasoning and statute. The response is something like this: the offender strikes against a sovereign body comprising the corporation of all persons as citizens. Criminal law reflects a social compact and codifies the norms of civil society, or indeed helps to shape that society, etc. By contrast, on this crucial matter, restorative justice voices are decidedly hushed. Conspicuously absent is a fully developed discussion of precisely what codes, morals or orders offenders violate, and who indeed is rightfully charged with making decisions regarding 'offending' behaviour beyond victim perception. We are clearly told that restorative justice focuses on such things as harm, obligation and participation, and one might surmise that the offender strikes against 'right relations'. We are also told that matters of guilt and innocence are not particularly relevant to problem-solving, future-directed restorative processes. However, if the governmentality refers to notions of the 'offender', with considerable effect, it is crucial to have some sense of several key questions. What makes one person who strikes against right relations criminal and another not so? Who defines what a crime is, and so licences the prospect of restorative justice processes? What is crime in restorative moral frameworks?

We have already had occasion to refer to Zehr's attempted reformulation of the categories of crime. As will be recalled, he offers a brief statement on the difference between criminal and restorative justice's respective understandings of crime, with the latter speaking of crime as a 'violation of people and relationships'.[6] At first blush, this may appear to offer a distinction of sorts, but on closer inspection it is simply too imprecise and vague to make the kind of claim in support of which it is mobilised. Take, for example, its unspecific use of the term 'violation'. There are many actions in everyday life that violate others or our relations with them; one might point to insults, harsh words, nasty comments, shunning, reprimands, angry gesticulations, failures to meet promises, etc. Doubtless such actions often violate others, but the question is, how and why should they be regarded as criminal? Clearly, this is not the case and, more to the point, Zehr's paradigm diametrically opposes any calls to move in any such direction. The issue is simply this: even if such definitions attempt to go beyond criminal justice definitions, their formulations are insufficiently precise to avoid designating relatively common events as criminal.

In the event, this lack of clarity produces significant contextual effects in context. For one, the governmentality neither actively contests criminal justice formulations of crime nor offers viable or well-developed alternatives to crime. As a result, the practices that bear its name (conferencing, mediation, panels, etc) end up taking for granted the very thing they are designed to contest. In other words, without a credible, precisely formulated notion of crime, restorative justice programs – perhaps unintentionally and by default – end up working with criminal justice definitions of 'crime'. In effect, we are left with this governmental rationality: the offender has committed a crime, as defined by adversarial courtroom practices, and restorative justice then deals with the harms of crime so defined. In short, without clear alternative formulations of what crime is, how it is to be defined, and indeed which agents are to do the defining, restorative governmentalities assume a default position of resting on criminal justice's adversarially produced definitions of crime and offender.

Consequently, even though supporters of restorative justice claim to offer an alternative to criminal justice agencies because of the way their processes approach, understand and deal with offenders, they are mobilised to deal with the harms of those

---

6   The complete citation to his earlier work reads thus: 'Crime is a violation of people and relationships. It creates obligations to make things right. Justice involves the victim, offender, and the community in a search for solutions which promote repair, reconciliation, and reassurance' (Zehr, 1990: 181).

legally defined as criminal. In the process, by default, they defer to criminal justice agencies to designate generally what crime is, and more specifically who is to be labelled criminal in a given context. These are the 'offenders' who populate restorative justice programs. Again, one glimpses the subtle way in which the *imitor* paradox replicates itself within restorative governmentalities. We are told that restorative justice is fundamentally different from criminal justice because of the ways in which it deals with offenders; however, by clinging to the identity of the criminal offender and by *not* redefining crime it relies upon criminal justice visions of crime and decisions about who is or is not an 'offender'. In so doing, it defers constitutively to the very criminal justice process it claims to repudiate.

One implication of the above paradox is to endorse crime as something of an absolute ontology devoid of the prior human judgments – by police, prosecutors and judges – that create the identity of criminal, or offender. In other words, by not analysing crime as a human construct, by allowing it to endure as an assumption that resides in silent shadows without analytical scrutiny, both criminal and restorative justice approaches perpetuate the myth that crime is somehow absolute and discoverable. Yet if it is anything, crime is an historically created ontology, not a fixed one. As such, it may be important for alternative calculations of justice not to assume the existence of crime, but to begin by assessing the contingent ways in which current criminal justice arrangements define crime.

Here one is brought to a potentially significant call to repoliticise crime-creating processes, and to recognise that calculations of justice do not have to centre themselves around 'crime'. That criminal justice institutions have for centuries tied justice to crime ought not to detract from the contingent horizons within which crime has always been formulated, to say nothing of the vastly differing ways in which criminal justice institutions have positioned themselves in relation thereto. In many ways, this points us in the direction of recovering a new politics of crime. For example, there may be much value in focusing attention on the gate-keeping or starting point where the process of creating a criminal identity begins: the moment at which accusers accuse others of a crime. This is the moment where 'strangers in our midst' are declared, and shifting cultural resources are mobilised to define outsiders from within. In any case, the performative rituals of crime creation and perpetuation, which include both restorative and criminal justice visions and agencies, are not to be ignored if an alternative calculation of justice is to be pursued.

The individual offender

In his influential analysis of modern disciplinary power relations, Foucault (1977) makes clear the ways in which rationalised administrative polities both create and use individuals as vehicles of disciplinary power. The argument, in part, is that as the massive spectacles intrinsic to medieval law and sovereign models of power become less effective at controlling an increasingly industrialised, urban population, so disciplinary powers instead replicate themselves through social networks and institutions to create normal subjects who are the bases of (normal) societies.[7] Despite the complex nuances of Foucault's argument, one point relevant to the present discussion concerns the ways in which disciplinary power works to create normal individuals through minute, subtle, normalising judgments, from subtle gestures of reward or punishment to grander (disciplinary) knowledge about the norm in a given observable field. A key implication of this insight is the notion that individuals – and especially free individuals – are not the opposite of, but central to, the perpetuation of power in modern societies.

This basic idea is worth keeping in mind when one considers that restorative governmentalities not only focus their efforts on self-governing entities, but also designate the offender as an individual identity. The assumption here is that crime and offending ought always to be considered in individual terms as violations against other people; that is, crime and its harm is to be conceptualised largely as an individual matter. Restorative justice processes may include community members (again as individuals), and make references to community integration and even change, but this in no way detracts from its emphasis on requiring the participation of offenders as *individuals* in its various processes and programs. All images of crime and harm centre on the offender as an individual identity who is obliged to confront harm and make responsible amends. At this point, traces of disciplinary power are clearly evident in restorative justice contexts.

---

7 Elsewhere I have discussed this approach in more detail in relation to community mediation: see Pavlich (1996a, 1996b).

This focus on the individual as one who 'strikes against' replicates the *imitor* paradox insofar as criminal justice's narrowed ways of dealing crime too rely mostly on individual designations of criminality. It is worth repeating a salient point. Restorative governmentalities in some places distance themselves from the individually focused dispositions of criminal justice, by including the community as a central stakeholder in matters of justice; however, they mostly also duplicate the criminal justice *modus operandi* of dealing with offences individually, singly. For example, hate crimes centred on race or ethnicity, or (as noted) sexual harassment/assault cases, some property crime, etc, emanate from conflicts and struggles that incarnate broad socio-political strategies in context. These strategies are sometimes abbreviated as patriarchy, racial inequality, class inequity, global poverty, and so on. However, calls for justice to address such broad strategic envelopes by focusing on individuals yield particular problems. It is difficult, for instance, to envisage how focusing on reforming individual offenders in local conferences is ever likely to grapple with, name and indeed resist the broad political strategies that both foreshadow and create given criminal events and their participants. The broad strategic tendencies nurture the very identities that are – in the politics of criminal justice – further elaborated upon as the 'offenders' that present before restorative conferences. Dealing with the politically generated individuals as offenders does not so much resist as entrench the wider power envelopes surrounding justice environments.

So, by replicating a criminal justice process which individualises offenders, restorative governmentalities narrow their own transformative potentials inordinately to reforming, reintegrating and restoring individual offenders, victims and individuals within communities. Despite the claims to develop (reform) communities, most programs focus on restoring individual offenders to the very social settings whose strategic envelopes and power differentials generated the identities that brought them into conflict with the law in the first place. This quiet irony may be recognised by those restorative justice advocates who acknowledge the importance of communal change,[8] but the force of this recognition is annulled by a

---

8   See Morris (2000) and Bush and Folger (1994).

persistent tendency to focus restorative processes on the individual offender.

The bearer of harm

Returning to the classical and positivist images of the offender within criminal justice terrains, one is struck by the degree to which both frameworks hold the individual to account for crime and any harms thereby produced. To be sure, their reasons for so doing differ from one to another, but not their emphasis on the offender. For classical approaches, the rational, pleasure-seeking offender – coupled perhaps with the failure of erstwhile deterrence measures – explains why people commit crimes. Neo-classical versions may rely less on notions of pleasure, but free, rational calibration is very much part of their understandings of criminal offending. Positivist formulations posit individual (biological/psychological) nature as the reason for criminal offending. Ultimately, however, both identify the individual offender as the source of criminal harm. It is therefore this individual who must be punished in direct proportion to the crime, and/or treated through various measures to rehabilitate him/her.

Against both these formulations,[9] restorative governmentalities claim not to focus as much on the offender's guilt as on the harms that led them to commit crimes, the harm they generate as a result of the crime, and the harm they experience from so offending. However, as emphasised, the primary image associated with the offender, and the reason why it is important for them to participate in restorative processes, is this: they must take responsibility, and make amends, for the harms that their offending produces. Shame and apology often emerge as concepts for offenders to embrace as they prepare to be reintegrated into communities; this underscores the basic view that it is the individual offender who is responsible for generating harm. In this respect, at least, there is a fundamentally homologous logic at play in restorative and criminal justice approaches – one that identifies the individual offender as the bearer of harm produced by crime.

---

9 See Johnstone (2002) for a discussion of the way in which these frameworks are contrasted with restorative justice.

The *imitor* paradox is reproduced in a somewhat oblique way here. As seen, restorative governmentalities claim to approach the offender quite differently from criminal justice approaches to the offender. He or she is held directly accountable and responsible to those who are hurt by crime – victim and community – rather than to impersonal laws, judges or juries. This, as noted, requires offenders to be responsible in far more consequential ways than is required when one faces up to the court and takes its punishments. Despite this difference, in so 'responsiblising' offenders, restorative justice governmentalities defer to a deeply entrenched criminal justice precept that posits the individual as a criminal. However one elects to define crime's harm – as a violation of law, person, communities or social relations – the source of that harm is located in one identity: the individual offender. Restorative justice thus claims to be different, again by deferring to fundamental tenets within the very approach it seeks to transcend.

There are consequential implications of the paradox here, especially when coupled to the notion that crime is effectively (by default) assumed to be a juridical decision. By implicitly accepting criminal justice designations of crime, and placing the responsibility for harm almost exclusively on offenders, restorative governmentalities join state counterparts in eschewing the possibility that great harms are very often introduced by criminal laws themselves. In some cases, for example, it is the designation of crime itself that generates the harm which an *alternative* calculation might rightly be expected to name. One could cite various examples. Consider the magnitude of the harms yielded by, say, Apartheid criminal laws – the criminalisation of those without passes to 'white areas', the criminalisation of 'mixed' relations, the criminalisation of protest, and so on. Though one could cite many other examples in this and other contexts (homosexuality laws), and across time, the point being made is not that the designation of crime through law is always harmful. It is only that, so long as the governmentality *assumes* harm to be generated by criminal offenders, it not only replicates the political logic of criminal justice but dangerously turns away from analysing the prospect that specific designations of crime are at times extremely harmful in their own right.

In addition, and by extension, approaching the offender as the main bearer of harm also deflects questions of justice away from wider power relations that might be as harmful as the act committed. Restorative justice governmentalities do in places recognise this issue, as noted, but it receives relatively short shrift. In efforts not to exonerate offenders from taking responsibility for the harms produced by their crime, restorative justice advocates do not dwell on how they propose to conceptualise the harms that broad power arrangements bring to criminal events. Braithwaite (2002) and Zehr (2002) usefully allude to such power formations, but focusing restorative justice on processes that locate harm as the domain of individual offenders does not open one up to a politics of crime and justice beyond legal terrain. As such, a laudable call to expand criminal justice beyond the narrowly defined limits of courtroom justice is not fully heeded. The potential for an alternative calculation of justice to work outside of the concepts and assumptions provided by criminal justice systems thus remains underdeveloped.

In sum, the *imitor* paradox replicates itself in three main ways in restorative justice governmentalities directed to offenders: by implicitly adopting images of crime supplied by criminal justice systems; by focusing on offenders as individuals; and by seeing offenders as the main source of harm. Throughout the discussion of offenders, it is important to recall that, despite everything, restorative justice processes aim to expunge the identity of 'offender'. Restorative governmentalities attempt to reduce crime through rituals in which offenders are empowered to participate in their own reformation, and to restore right relations. One might here refer back to Bentham's indirect control that seeks to shape the will of subjects, their motivations; restorative governmentalities see the importance of shaping offender motivations away from the destruction of harms, and towards acting in ways that will enable their integration into communities. However, one can detect the omniscient shadow of direct control prowling silently but restlessly at the foundations of indirect control, delimiting the calculations around such precepts as crime and offender. There is much to learn from this when trying to think through what it means to posit alternative visions of either justice or control.

Chapter 5
The State of Restored Communities

Most restorative justice proponents seek restorative processes that will simultaneously grapple with crime's aftermath and nurture strong communities. Since the community provides a pivotal means of distinguishing restorative and state approaches to justice, it is not surprising that the appeal to community is so ubiquitous in context, even though various understandings of community populate restorative governmentalities. Here, the community signifies a collective paradise lost, to be regained through the healing, the relational transformations that restorative processes promise. This backdrop of the ideal community is assumed in context, resonating with broader cultural tendencies.

Bauman phrases a rhetorical question that reflects this assumed culture succinctly:

> Who would not wish to live among friendly and well-wishing people whom one could trust and on whose words and deeds one could rely? For us in particular – who happen to live in ruthless times, times of competition and one-upmanship, when people around seem to keep their cards close to their chests and few people seem to be in a hurry to help us, when in reply to our cries for help we hear admonitions to help ourselves, when only the banks eager to mortgage out possessions are smiling and wishing to say 'yes' ... the word community sounds sweet (2001: 2–3).

It is perhaps for this reason, he continues, that:

> The word 'community' ... feels good: whatever the word 'community' may mean, it is good 'to have a community', 'to be in a community'. Company or society can be bad; but not the *community*. Community, we feel, is always a good thing ... 'community' is nowadays another name for a paradise lost – but one to which we dearly hope to return, and so we feverishly seek the roads that may bring us there (2001: 1–3).

The emotional appeal of community within the uncertainties of our ethos is especially compelling, and may explain why community-based initiatives are nowadays accepted as a panacea for all sorts of ills, including the ills alleged to accompany courtroom justice. Such is the broader cultural horizon that sympathetically embraces a governmentality depicting its processes and techniques as 'home-grown' and community-based, drawing on a history far more ancient – and so presumably more authentic – than the punitive impositions of state justice.

In appealing to such primordial images to distinguish itself from criminal justice, restorative justice invokes a concept of community as intrinsically beyond, in excess of, the state and its justice. The present chapter will now explore the more influential – and often implicit – images of community played on by restorative justice governmentalities. Following that, I examine how the *imitor* paradox is replicated through attempts to distinguish restorative from criminal justice by appealing to visions of community that are closely aligned with – if not largely created by – state agencies. Again, the paradox is instructive for thinking through what an alternative vision of justice might entail.

Restoring community

The New Zealand Ministry of Justice, where acclaimed youth justice programs were established, to much international attention, is unequivocal: 'Central to Restorative Justice is a recognition of community, rather than criminal justice agencies, as the prime site of control' (1995: 1). Sharpe echoes the sentiment: 'Restorative justice is community-based' (1998: 46); and Zehr expresses the view that, for restorative justice advocates, 'The justice process belongs to the community' (2002: 68). The founding place of community in restorative justice thus reverberates throughout the discourse.[1]

---

1 Located as it is at the heart of many restorative formulations, the very idea of community justice is not always distinguishable from its restorative kin. Attempts to do so render the nuance clear – restorative justice is said to involve formulations of 'communities' that parallel legal jurisdictions, whereas community justice supposedly involves 'neighbourhoods', being more directly 'reform' orientated (Crawford and Clear, 2003: 215). To be sure, many restorative justice advocates would contest this division; either way, community provides a defining attribute of restorative justice.

As a means of distinguishing restorative and adversarial processes of justice, the community functions to propagate restorative mentalities in various ways. In his analysis of this issue, Walgrave (2002b) identifies at least four purposes that the concept of community fulfils in restorative justice contexts:

(1) It extends notions of victim and offender, providing a collective framework from which to consider such subjects.

(2) The community provides a 'social' context that renders images and practices of 'restoration' meaningful (2002a: 75). The key point here is the relational domain that community provides outside the state, thus offering a way of distinguishing restorative from criminal justice.

(3) Community is also positioned as a 'secondary victim' to the extent that crime tears away its relational fabric, which also needs to be restored through healing processes. Referring back to Chapter 2, he is here referring to how communities are 'harmed' by crime.

(4) At the other end of the spectrum – and concerning the aim of the process – conceptions of a strong community are posited as the utopia, the valued goal of restorative justice.

As I see it, restorative governmentalities focus a great deal of attention on the first three whilst assuming the fourth through its proffered images. That assumed background status is also implicit below, where I focus attention on the first three.

Victims, offenders and their communities

Within restorative governmentalities, the victims and offenders of crime are viewed as members of one or other shared community. They hail, so the reasoning goes, from various collective relations that nurture, support and help to create them as particular sorts of individuals. The criminal action of an offender on a victim has affected both of their identities to some degree, as well as wider collective relations.[2] With these particular criminal relational complexes as a focus, restorative justice governmentalities consider victims, offenders, family members and all those affected by a crime as forming a micro-

---

2 Hence, as Sharpe puts it, 'There is a fundamental need to rebuild the sense of community that is eroded by crime' (1998: 46).

community of sorts. Deploying restorative measures within those communities, micro and macro, is viewed as invigorating community participation and empowering affected parties to develop communal responses to the aftermath of crime. By empowering victims, offenders and affected people to deal with the crime, restorative justice governmentalities claim to strengthen communities and operate outside of state justice domains. But what precisely does such a community entail?

For some, the community is best understood as a group of people united because they share a defined geographical place or space (eg, Sharpe, 1998). 'Neighbourhood justice' advocates especially tend to focus on developing specific local forms of justice tied to place.[3] A related 'community justice' champions the importance of developing justice within the 'neighbourhood', conceived as a locus where intersecting lives converge; they focus particularly on reforms that would nurture democratically strong communities (Crawford and Clear, 2003; Clear and Karp, 2002). In contrast to the idea of community as contingent upon place, other formulations appeal to broader communitarian precepts where the community is viewed as the product of relations between people based on common interests, values, goals and aspirations (for example, extended families, sports clubs, community leagues, hiking clubs, and so on). The underlying theme is some sort of union between specific groups, broadly *'a group of people linked by belief, interest, or commitment, or by membership in an organization or institution'* (Sharpe, 1998: 46; emphasis in original). From this vantage, community exists only where individuals perceive that they are 'connected', or linked, to others.

To take another example, McCold and Wachtel ask and respond to the question of community in this way:

> What is community? Community is a feeling, a perception of connectedness – personal connectedness both to other individual human beings and to a group. Building community, then, involves building bonds between human beings. Where there is no perception of connectedness among a group of people, there is no community (2003: 295).

By this definition, community members are required to identify with one another through a certain connectedness, a perception

---

3 For example, Kurki (1999); see also Abel (1982) and Hofrichter (1987).

that they are somehow fundamentally unified, together, etc. Each individual must identify him/herself with a defined grouping. This ephemeral quality of identification through connection with others is essential to this formulation of community. To the extent that restorative justice processes encourage participants to experience and develop their perceptions of connectedness, it becomes a vehicle for enabling the most basic component of communal life.

In these communitarian renderings, restorative justice helps people to attain the ideal of community by encouraging members to interact and feel connected to one another. The dialogical dimensions of restorative processes are key. Justice emerges as a way of 'empowering' stakeholders harmed by a criminal event to negotiate restorative outcomes. It is designed to help them perceive a greater connection to other members of their communities in order to 'respond to and prevent crime and wrongdoing' (McCold and Wachtel, 2003: 296). In a related fashion, Zehr argues that:

> In practice, restorative justice has tended to focus on 'communities of care' or micro-communities ... For restorative justice, the key questions are: 1) who in the community cares about these people or this offence, and 2) how can we involve them in this process? (2002: 27–28)

The image of relatively transitory 'communities of care' that emerge around a given set of circumstances is influential within restorative governmentalities.[4] These 'communities' are seen to develop around a criminal event to help and support those involved, especially victims but also offenders.

Against this 'community of care' idea, other supporters propose a perspective that conceptualises the community as essential to vibrant civil societies. Here, the community is considered a crucial ingredient for creating the 'people' who are necessary to and capable of making informed political choices in working republican democracies (Strang and Braithwaite, 2001). Here, the community is envisaged as a collective manifestation of spontaneous interactions between free individuals outside – but vital to the democratic functions of – formal state institutions

---

4   For an analysis of this point, see Johnstone (2002); for further examples, see Bazemore (1998) and Galaway and Hudson (1996); for a critique thereof, see Shearing (2001).

(Braithwaite, 2002; Shonholtz, 1988/89). Community participation is recruited to the cause of democracy as a way of nurturing civil society's active involvement in responding to harmful conflict.

Finally, still other proponents of restorative justice envisage the community as an entirely amorphous idea, a symbolic or imagined representation that both reflects and creates group identities. As an imagined idea, a symbol, the idea of community serves to represent, and offer an ideal blueprint for, our everyday interactions with others. On this view, restorative justice is enlisted to *transform* interpersonal relations for the better, and to provide a vocabulary for envisioning harmonious, peaceful communities (Pranis, 2003; Morris, 2000; Bush and Folger, 1994).

Although by no means exhaustive, these diverse conceptions demonstrate various understandings of community invoked within restorative governmentalities.[5] The imprecise, indistinct and competing definitions of community do not provide a singular vision, but the assumption that such an entity does exist regardless allows restorative justice to distinguish itself from state criminal justice. The community is assumed to be a self-evident ontological entity somehow more familiar, immediate and basic to everyday human relations than the sorts of interactions required by state-based criminal justice institutions. It is an *a priori* feature of restorative justice – the victims of crime, as well as the offending perpetrators, are by definition seen as inhabiting the (variously defined) communities to which restorative justice processes are attached, and from which resources are drawn.

Furthermore, many advocates see their emphasis on community as a means of resisting a tendency in contemporary life to erode communal attachments as a result of a pervasive and 'excessive' individualism.[6] Increasing levels of crime are seen to be symptomatic of that tendency. For instance, McCold and Wachtel argue that 'Against a tide of individualism and a perceived decline of community life, we long for a sense of connectedness in our lives and a sense of safety in our neighbourhoods' (2003: 296). These restorative justice advocates see the task of rebuilding communities as key to collective safety, and that requires the active participation of individuals – victims,

---

5 For more on the general debates surrounding the concept community, see Amit (2002) and Cohen (2002).
6 See McCold and Wachtel (2003: 295) and Braithwaite (2002: 142ff).

offenders, family members, and other 'stakeholders' – to deal with crime.[7] The basic idea is this:

> ... when community members in these different roles are brought together, they develop new relationships. These relationships continue to evolve and create other relationships and even whole networks, which then generate new activities or action with respect to other community matters. At the same time, individuals feel more connected to and care about their community (Kurki, 2003: 308).

Consequently, community strength is tied to the active involvement of *individual* subjects who do not simply leave the state to deal with crime – instead, they wrest control back from the state and use restorative processes to find lasting solutions to criminal events. In the process, they forge alliances and ties that strengthen community bonds. Thus, in this schema, the strong community comprises active, participating, responsible individual citizens empowered to be directly involved in justice processes previously usurped by the state's criminal justice system. Restorative justice processes must in essence be 'dialogue-driven', explicitly requiring that individual participants actively contribute to mediations, conferences, panels and the like (Umbreit, 2001: xlii). Individual active participation is crucial, because – as we have already noted – 'Stakeholder deliberation determines what restoration means in context' (Braithwaite, 2002: 11). Such individual participation and dialogue in the restorative justice process is deemed crucial to redressing the effects of crime, because 'Our identities are embedded in our stories, so the recreation of meaning requires the "re-storying" of our lives' (Zehr, 2002: 24).

Strong communities are thus residual by-products of active individual participants who voluntarily take charge of restoring themselves and righting relationships distorted by criminal events. And restorative justice processes deploy forums that encourage affected parties to be so involved. Restorative justice then 'draws from community resources and, in turn, contributes to the building and strengthening of community' (Zehr, 2002: 68). Kurki (2003: 309) elaborates further by noting several reasons 'to expect that restorative justice practices will work better than do most other community building efforts'. She argues that restorative justice requires the 'direct participation' of 'ordinary people' who reclaim the authority to make decisions about an

---

7   See Zehr (2002), Bush and Folger (1994) and Pranis (2003).

event without the intervention of criminal justice agencies. In addition, she argues, restorative justice's focus on domination-free discourse, wide-ranging dialogue, consensus, concrete problem-solving, victim-offender support and respect for all parties enables opportunities for gatherings that are likely to strengthen communities.

In parenthesis, one might note that, despite a lack of definitional clarity, restorative justice governmentalities hold firm to their assumption that the community does actually exist and that its contours are amenable to discovery.[8] Yet, as Walgrave notes:

> Building on communities for developing restorative responses to crime, as many do, presupposes that a community really exists, and this is not self-evident (2002b: 76).

We shall have reason to return to this matter, but it is perhaps important to mention it here in passing.

Restoring a spontaneous, voluntary and non-state relational domain

Restorative visions of community also make sense of the foundational question that could legitimately be levelled at the discourse: what is to be restored? We examined this question previously in Chapter 2 in relation to healthy orders. However, in the present context, the discourse evokes community relations damaged by crime as in need of restoration. Furthermore, in at least one influential strand of thought, the restored community is deemed essential to the functioning of effective liberal democracies. The idea that individuals in civil society constitute the 'people' of a democracy is, of course, present in many versions of liberal politics. However, this image of democracy presumes that the state derives from, and is ultimately responsible to, domains of freedom that grant individuals the liberty to make key choices in their lives (including the basic choice to elect representatives who form a given state assembly).

At the same time, from this view, the state acts as a coercive safeguard to the possibility that particular subjects might decide to exercise their freedom in ways that seriously hurt others. As Strang and Braithwaite put it:

---

8   The lack of a precise formulation of community is echoed in wider debates around the notion – see Amit (2002) generally and especially Cohen (2002).

> From a republican normative perspective, it may be that what
> one wants is for both state and civil society to be strong so that
> each can act as a check and balance on the other (2001: 9).

The perhaps dialectical relation between state and civil society is
one of the foundations of (republican) democracy, because the
latter is premised on the assumption that there is a unique
domain in which individuals can spontaneously and freely
interact with others; active participation that encourages
thoughtful, caring, civic-minded and domination-free
deliberation amongst political subjects is deemed to foster viable
liberal democracies. The latter require something like a public
sphere in which subjects can 'freely' deliberate on political
choices in the absence of state intervention.[9] Restorative justice
provides an example of precisely such a public sphere because it
operates in the community, a supposedly spontaneous relational
domain that provides the ground for a robust civil society.

Related to the above, a cornerstone of restorative justice's
ability to secure strong communities involves getting individuals
to take responsibility for redressing given criminal circumstances.
As Braithwaite puts it:

> Active responsibility is the virtue of taking responsibility for
> putting things right. The democratic idea of the restorative justice
> conference is that a space is created in which all participants
> might exhibit the virtue of taking active responsibility for putting
> things right, for preventing recurrence ... restorative justice is
> about nurturing the taking of active responsibility, especially by
> offenders who are given the most compelling reasons to do so by
> the discussion of the consequences of a crime (2002: 129).

With the above in mind, the vibrant community is taken to
consist of individual citizens who have learned to become
actively responsible for dealing with conflict and crime, without
depending on state justice. The strong community is envisaged
as a collection of active, voluntarily participating, responsible,
dialogically open and engaged stakeholders who include

---

9   As Strang and Braithwaite argue, 'If one of the values of restorative justice
    is to enrich democracy, to implement participatory deliberation in an
    important domain of people's lives, then it follows that a process is
    needed in which all stakeholders have an opportunity to speak' (2001:
    11–12).

offenders, victims and family as well as affected community members. These individuals comprise the foundations of restorative justice with its emphasis on community resolutions and the aspiration to a thriving liberal democracy in which the powers of (or indeed dependency upon) the state are radically limited.

This emphasis on community as a cornerstone of liberal democracy is also apparent in communitarian mediation discourses.[10] Shonholtz (1978, 1984, 1988/89), for instance, notes the importance of community mediation in developing community participation, and thereby encouraging civic engagement. Mediation is said to 'improve the quality of community life through more direct citizen participation, reduced community tension and increased community problem-solving skills' (Peachey and Tymec, 1989: 43). Contemporary writers who note the importance of mobilising communities in the justice process reiterate the point.[11] As with the 'normative republican' theories, these approaches endorse developing active, voluntary, direct and spontaneous community participation amongst members. They also enlist restorative justice as a key site through which communities must take back responsibility and control of conflict, grappling directly with specific criminal events.[12]

So, the governmentalities at hand distinguish between state and non-state, community domains. As a community-based approach, restorative justice claims to occupy voluntary domains outside, and beyond the immediate reach of, coercive state apparatuses. Specifically, this putative distinction between the voluntarism of community and coercion of state reinforces the previously discussed idea that restorative justice be considered legitimate precisely because it is an alternative to (and is so untainted by the manifest failures of) the anonymous values and adversarial processes of the state criminal justice system:

---

10 See Pavlich (1996a: 57 ff).

11 Eg, Pranis (2003), Umbreit (2001), Morris (2000) and Sharpe (1998).

12 See, generally, Johnstone (2003), Weitekamp and Kerner (2002), Consedine and Bowen (1999), Sharpe (1998), Consedine (1995) and Christie (1977).

> By excluding the known and immediate community in favour of
> its remote and anonymous legal representations, the state
> entrenches division, leaves conflicts open, and misses critical
> opportunities for compromise, resolution and restoration
> (McLaughlin *et al*, 2003: 7).

The point is that restorative discourses formulate values and
processes of justice as essentially of the community, and thus as
something distinct from state justice domains.

Healing community harms

Although we have noted the importance that restorative justice
governmentalities attach to individual harms caused by crime,
they also recognise that crime extends beyond interpersonal
relations. In particular, the 'community' is singled out as one of
the entities simultaneously harmed by, and responsible for,
crime: 'Crime also brings harm to the community, and is a
responsibility of the community' (Sharpe, 1998: 46). Restorative
justice seeks to restore communities, and enable them to take
direct responsibility for solving the harm generated by crime.
Especially notable in this regard is the view that crime yields a
profoundly destructive sense of communal insecurity.

Most functional communities, so the argument goes, can only
work when their members have a basic sense of safety and
security, held together by the fabric of well woven, balanced,
harmonious community relations. When people become aware
that a crime has been committed in their midst, they are made
acutely aware of their vulnerability as potential victims. This, in
turn, produces fear and often distrust amongst members; it also
disturbs a presumed order of life – exacting profound emotional
costs. As Morris argues:

> … the wider community is affected by every breach in the social
> fabric. The fear and anger and a sense of hopelessness escalate
> (2000: 254).[13]

To the extent that crime eats away at collective sentiment, it
destroys the very fabric of communal life. Consequently,

---

13 She adds to that, 'The existing justice system offers nothing more than a
process to lock up and further damage and in rage of person defined as
bad, while doing nothing significant for victims or for public safety. Far
from protecting the public, it maximizes the charms of recidivism by
increasing offender alienation and anger, and decreasing the charms of
any healthy integration into the community' (Morris, 2000: 254).

restorative governmentalities argue that criminal harms within a community generate unique needs. For instance, an affected community needs to deal with crime in order to 'restore' a sense of its safety, security, integrity and strength (Shonholtz, 1988/89). Communities decimated by crime need to be empowered and rebuilt to prevent future damaging events such as crime. A sense of community should be nurtured such that members come to recognise their constitutive responsibilities to each other for expunging crime-generated harm. By valuing and encouraging the active participation of community members who are affected by crime, restorative justice sees itself as addressing the needs created by criminal acts, by restoring community strength.

There is also a more deeply committed communitarian strand to restorative governmentalities which acknowledges that crime may be harm-producing but is also the unfortunate yield, or symptom, of problems within a community, or indeed of a problematic community. From this vantage, many contemporary communities are seen to be in disarray, even decay, and so are themselves partly responsible for crimes committed. Such communities must take responsibility for crime in their midst, recovering a basic responsibility usurped by the growth of formal criminal justice systems (Weitekamp, 2003; Zehr, 1990). Having been stripped of the means to deal with crime, so we are told, many communities are now so weakened that they cannot take responsibility for criminality within. Responding actively to criminal events could encourage battered communities to confront their responsibilities for crime (as was the case before the introduction of the modern legal system), and provide a catalyst for needed reforms to strengthen communal ties (Shonholtz, 1988/89). So, weakened community ties must be rebuilt so as not to harm people, and so perpetually spawn new offenders. As a result, various analysts call for restorative justice to transform communities to: provide 'transformative justice' (in Bush and Folger's (1994) terms); promote fundamental social reform (Morris, 2000); reclaim strong moral ties (Consedine, 1995); or strengthen grassroots democratic traditions (Strang and Braithwaite, 2001). In each case, the community is portrayed as both nurturer and recipient of criminal harm, requiring fundamental communitarian reforms to generate strong community ties that could lessen, if not entirely eradicate, crime.

To reiterate, then, within restorative justice governmentalities, three important functions of the concept of 'community' outline images that define restorative practices as distinctly outside state justice domains. Although defined in different ways, the community is uniformly held as a domain separate from the state and whose strength derives from the active participation of individual victims, offenders and other affected stakeholders. The importance of this entity for vital democracies is emphasised, as is the idea that crime is harmful to its relational fabric – the healing of which demands that attention be paid to unique interrelational needs generated in context.

Imitor, aporia and community states

The quest for community-based processes allows advocates to allege that restorative justice is separate from state-based, courtroom justice, thereby underscoring the importance of maintaining the 'community' as an ontologically distinct terrain for restorative governmentalities. If restorative justice is uniquely different because it deals with the aftermath of crime in the 'community', then it follows that the latter entity ought to exist independently of state agencies. However, the *imitor* paradox surfaces here in at least three connected ways. First, attempts to delineate an autochthonous community are undermined by a reliance on state agencies to provide the necessary auspice of communal being. The point is clearly highlighted by McCold and Wachtel in the following statement. They claim that community-based, restorative processes do provide:

> ... effective informal social control mechanisms. Where these are not available, the government has the responsibility to provide them ... Government, however, cannot effectively address crime without the moral authority and informal social control provided by community (2003: 301).

The state is therefore called upon to provide for its own communal grounding, thereby replicating the *imitor* paradox in context. Secondly, restorative communities form around, and in response to, prior delineations of crime. Here, the hidden hand of criminal justice arranges the foundations of restorative governmentalities directed to community. Thirdly, community development is predicated upon the active participation of at least two key figures defined through criminal justice notions – the individual victim and offender. Let us explore each of these in turn.

Ontological instabilities

Interestingly, within restorative justice discourses, the absolute existence of community is more or less assumed. However, conspicuously absent is a correspondingly uniform, or clear-cut, definition thereof. As Walgrave observes, 'Nowhere is the community defined in any concrete way, even when explicit attempts are made cope with the criticism of non-definition' (2002b: 74–75). As he notes further, the matter is chronic, for 'community' cannot be made 'concrete'; it is simply 'too vague a concept' to perform the functions that supporters of restorative justice would want it to do.[14] Is this so? Consider Bazemore and Griffiths' response to this sort of challenge, and their attempt to formulate a precise, concrete definition:

> Community may be defined, for example, as a neighbourhood, a church, a school, a labour union, a civic and fraternal organization, and extended family, an aboriginal band or tribe, a support group, or other entity (2003: 81).

One cannot help wondering whether these attempts to make the concept more concrete end up confirming rather than annulling the attendant vagaries to which Walgrave refers. Equally, Zehr's formulation, though more interesting, seems similarly poised:

> In practice, restorative justice has tended to focus on 'communities of care', or micro-communities. There are communities of *place* where people live near and interact with each other, but there are also networks of relationships that are not geographically defined (2002: 27).

The catchments are vast; perhaps too vast to enable, discursively, the sort of precision implied by the assumption that the community comprises an ontologically unified and independent entity.

Regardless, restorative justice advocates tend to position the community as spontaneous and voluntary collective domains

---

14 Ironically, the quandary is evinced by the very question: 'What is community?' Despite seeming to raise fundamental questions about the basis of community, the question begins by assuming the existence of the entity that it seeks to predicate. The discursive task involved with such a question is thus not to answer whether there is such a thing as community or not, but merely to define or describe its presumed nature. This enables the situation where the community's independent existence is assumed despite a notorious inability to define such an entity precisely.

that constitute the foundations of civil society. But does restorative justice put these domains into play? First, the notion that community is a spontaneous form of association is betrayed by the constructed organisation and rules that accompany all restorative justice programs. To be blunt, if the community were a spontaneous way of associating around a given criminal event, would it be necessary to arrange participation, organise program provision, or prescribe elaborate rules as a condition of participating in restorative justice? Secondly, it is not at all clear that participants voluntarily choose restorative justice processes. The 'choices' available to those involved with a criminal event are all too often Hobson's choices: restorative justice appears more as a lesser evil amongst difficult options before participants. The threat of coercion ('if you don't participate you must face the judge') often shadows the supposed voluntarism of some participants' choices.

If such worries militate against the idea of community as a stable, spontaneous ontology, the ubiquitous presence of state agents in restorative justice practices challenges the claim to independence from the state. We should not forget that state agencies all too often design, create, implement, sanction, finance, staff and select which cases to divert to restorative justice. They provide for restorative justice through diverse ministerial portfolios, and it is from these that community-based restorative justice often derives legitimacy, authority and resources. If the liberal power formations thereby actively engineer the 'spontaneous' and 'voluntary' collective domains whose aspirations they are supposed to reflect, they also embed such relations at the heart of restorative initiatives. This undermines claims that restorative justice's community is a stable ontology independent of state agency. Paradoxically, restorative justice's community may be championed as a spontaneous, voluntary foundation of liberal democracies, but the omniscient hand of state agency lies in the shadows of such lofty ideals. The *imitor* paradox surfaces in restorative communities that are constituted as independent of state justice precisely by depending on the constitutive provisions of state agency.

Crime's community

Restorative governmentalities address the idea of community as a response to criminal events. Regardless of whether community is mobilised as a geographical boundary, common interest, symbol, or around images of care, the precipitating moment of interest to restorative governmentalities is crime. That is, communities are examined largely in relation to how crime harms their relational fabric, and what can be done to restore them to some or other utopian ideal (as enunciated through the various definitions of community). By revolving around a criminal event, the idea of community in restorative governmentalities helps to confirm the absolute existence of crime. In so doing, the *imitor* paradox reproduces itself by deferring, fundamentally, to a founding concept of criminal justice, the very terrain from which restorative governmentalities claim independence.

As noted in Chapter 4, crime is assumed – by default – as that which is defined by criminal justice agencies. Even when advocates loosely aspire to alternate images of crime, their practical commitments and focus betray a rather more sustained attachment to crime as formulated through criminal justice practices. The *imitor* paradox does not absent itself from such commitments or practices; in addition, the implications of focusing community-based justice around criminal justice's images of crime are both consequential and several. By not challenging the primordial status accorded to legal definitions of crime, the governmentality does not raise questions about the very idea of crime (what is crime?), the value of clinging to crime as a viable concept for defining harm (does harm have to be a product of crime?), whether specific definitions of crime are themselves harmful, or indeed whether contemporary fascinations that amount to cultures of crime ought to be transcended. Though such basic questions might be traced as nascent to early 'informalism' critiques of criminal justice, the dramatic success of more recent restorative justice measures has occurred largely through amnesic subversions of their earlier critiques. Deploying restorative communities around the notion of 'crime', effectively enunciating crime's community, speaks of a grand appeasement in which restorative justice proponents claim a distinct identity from state justice, but do so by deploying their justice around – rather than against – founding precepts of the latter.

The community of victims and offenders

The age-old conundrum of the relationship between the one and the many, the individual and society or community, is in many ways constitutive of disciplines such as sociology. Within sociology, Durkheim for instance sought to contain 'methodological individualism' and to focus on the laws of 'the social'. Far from seeing the nature of individuals as determining the shape of society, collective being was deemed to have its own determinations, independent of individuals. Indeed, the individual was taken to be the product of particular kinds of societies. Consequently, to change society would require modifications directed specifically at the structures that created particular forms; in turn, these transformations affect the kinds of individuals produced. From this vantage, focusing reforms on the products of social structures – for example, individuals – could yield very limited collective changes, if any. Marx's theories of revolution, which explicitly repudiate the value of predicating revolutionary social transformations on liberally conceived individuals, provide the archetypical case at hand for the point.

This conundrum makes an appearance in restorative justice discourses in a somewhat diametrically opposed fashion. Although the community appears as a utopian aspiration, particular individual identities are placed as the founding units of communities. Specifically, victims (primarily) and offenders are placed at the centre of restorative justice communities designated to deal with the aftermath of crime. Restorative processes empower victims to become active participants in seeking justice, to articulate the needs generated by the harms of crime; equally, they attempt to empower offenders to face, and make amends for, the damage resulting from their offences. Their active participation, moreover, in seeking to heal the harms of crime is postulated as developing and restoring strong communities.

Recall that restorative governmentalities claim to be distinguishable from criminal justice approaches because of their emphasis on the role of the community when dealing with the aftermath of crime. Yet, ironically, the strength of that very community is also taken to reside with the active participation of the self-same individual subjects that inhabit criminal justice processes – the victim, offender and (arguably) the affected community members. Granted, these subjects are given different roles to play, but their ascribed identity as individual victims and offenders remains remarkably consistent in both criminal and restorative justice processes. This *imitor* paradox undermines restorative claims to deploy essentially community-based processes that are uniquely different from criminal justice rationales and practices. Clearly, spectres of the *imitor* paradox appear when the image of community used to differentiate restorative from criminal justice rests on empowering identities of key figures – victims and offenders – as defined within the courtroom. Imitating key identities used by the very justice from which they seek to be distinguished, restorative governmentalities overlay their notions of community firmly on conceptual terrains staked by criminal justice. In other words, the strength of this community is thus paradoxically used to signal the distinctiveness of a restorative justice founded upon the active participation of such adversarial *personae* as victims and offenders as the basis of strong, democratic, communal formations.

The *imitor* paradox also implies at least two further layers of paradox in this area of restorative governmentalities. First, as indicated, the purported emphasis on *community* concerns is explicitly championed – not unlike criminal justice arenas – through the benefits of *individual* participation (see Carson 2004a; 2004b). Adding a layer to this paradox, one might argue that restorative processes can only achieve anything like success where collective ties are already strong. It is difficult to conceive how family group conferences, with their individual foci, could effectively 'restore' violence-torn ghettos to communitarian havens when those collective identities are often defined through complex forms of gang warfare and violence. If this is so, then any attempts to 'rebuild' communities using the very processes that assume the presence of developed communities in the first place are likely to be fraught.

Secondly, there is a paradox buried in the aspiration to community as an intrinsically valued moral utopia. If the community provides a figurative home, a relational respite from state justice formations, there is also a dark side to this utopia. Derrida captures the thrust of the point succinctly:

> If by community one implies, as is often the case, a harmonious group, consensus, and fundamental agreement beneath phenomena of discord or war, then I don't believe in it very much and I sense in it as much threat as promise (Derrida, 1995: 355).

I have elsewhere echoed Derrida's concerns about the dangers of entrenching closed visions of community through restorative practices.[15] Aside from the parochialism, exclusions, prohibitions and segregations associated with fixed notions of community, grounding restorative governmentalities in community harbours a profoundly troubling inability to avoid dangerous exclusions. Nazi, Stalinist, Apartheid or other regimes that strive to create fixed borders, impervious boundaries, in community members' imaginings palpably symbolise this threat. Of course, not all evocations of community necessarily lead to totalitarian disasters; the point is that governmental rationales that do not explicitly focus responsibility on those who they exclude are not well positioned to guard against despotic exclusions. As Cohen (2001) usefully indicates, the processes that separate insiders from outsiders to form a given community all too often anaesthetise newly defined insiders, preventing them from empathising with the excluded.

However, there can be no such thing as a universal community, since communities define themselves precisely through the delimiting of borders. A community's members are always distinguished from outsiders; to identify any given community is to distinguish insiders from those who live outside that community – strangers, offenders, etc (Bauman, 1997). As a result, the threat of totalitarianism threatens communities who see their basic responsibilities as revolving around included members. The unity (*unum*), being with (*com*), the identity, the common, is made present through successful exclusions that erect limits, brace borders, specify boundaries. Far less (if any) emphasis is placed on being responsible to those cast as non-members. It is perhaps not surprising that community should be related to the Latin *municeps* (from whence we have 'municipal'), which denoted those who could count themselves as citizens of a Roman city (the *municipium*), but who were not permitted to be magistrates (Ayto, 1990). Restorative justice's community is like the citizen who serves the state but not as an entirely sanctioned official. The walled city may keep strangers out through the coercions of law's empires, but the community assists by carving supportive limits through its unique governance.

This is community's secret: communities are identified – implicitly or explicitly – by exclusion. Identifying a community

---

15 Pavlich (2001, 2002a and 2002b). See also Carson (2004a, 2004b) for a thoughtful review of the concepts promise and pitfalls of community aspiration in crime control arenas.

thus may enable offenders to face their responsibilities to victims and communities, but they are far less emphatic that communities should have responsibilities towards those who are excluded. Derrida describes the problem thus:

> Once you grant some privilege to gathering and not to dissociating, you leave no room for the other, for the radical otherness of the other, for the radical singularity of the other (Derrida, 1997: 14).

There is, one might say, a short leap from the promises of bordered community life to the claim that one community is superior to, and therefore uniquely capable of deciding the fate of, others. The latter hazard provides a fertile breeding ground for the most perilous, irresponsible and tyrannical of exclusions. To the extent that restorative governmentalities emphasise boundaries and borders around communities, they are implicated in possible totalitarian effects – even if unintended and unforeseen – that may arise when a responsibility to the excluded is ignored.

Perhaps this dimension leads us to another question:

> ... how the community can remain a place for communality while at the same time being an open, interrupted community that is respectful of difference and resists the closure implicit within totalitarianism and immanentism (Critchley, 1992: 219).

Several commentators have responded by attempting to conceive of unsettled, open communities (eg, Agamben, 1993; Nancy, 1991; Corlett, 1989). These analysts recognise that the appeal to community is always an ethical, prescriptive matter that demands a continuously open-ended, changing, and future-directed aspiration of how to be with others. Such aspirations within restorative governmentalities are all too often compromised by the tendency to close off around fixed images of crime, healing and consensual communities.

In sum, then, the community is never universal (a universal community is meaningless); communities are always defined by delimitation. As a result, they include and exclude specific members, making them fundamentally exclusive to some degree. The basic responsibility and accountability of restorative communities, however defined, is to its members (see Woolford and Ratner, 2003). The danger of totalitarianism lurks in the shadows of collective formations that define themselves in this fashion, especially when they define responsibility as a matter of individual offenders recognising and making amends for the harm they cause to victims and communities. Ironically, although often championed as intrinsically homely, hospitable and good, communities by their very structure are exclusive and thus fraught with danger (that is, there is as much promise as there is a totalitarian threat contained therein). Could this mean that it may be possible to calculate justice beyond community, or at least state-based visions thereof?

Chapter 6
Justice Anew?

In 1832, a Member of the British Parliament, one Thomas Babington Macaulay, is reputed to have uttered these telling words: 'People crushed by law,' he warned, 'have no hopes but from power. *If laws are their enemies, they will be enemies to law.*'[1] He thus intoned the importance of 'incorporating' new groups into law, subordinating all parties to state power. Since his time, the terms of different 'incorporations' of new subjectivities have been orchestrated by law's ability to predefine limited conceptual horizons, mentalities that render particular incorporations practicable. Successive historical waves of legal reform suggest an irregular yet astonishingly robust quality to legal hegemonies – even though describing the situation as absorption by stealth might accord too hypostatised an identity and agency to 'law', legal fields do display a chameleon-like ability to assimilate even the most determined of contenders to justice. Restorative justice has proved to be, despite the critical promise of its early incarnations, no match for that capricious old fox which is assembled under the banner of criminal justice. By virtue of the diverse replications of the *imitor* paradox, through which restorative justice both governs and is governed, restorative governmentalities have fallen prey to the faint incorporations of criminal justice empires. This book has alluded to various governmental nuances of such subtle integration and absorption.

Yet it is important to stress that there may be little hope of escaping some degrees of incorporation, some measure of the *imitor*'s paradoxical environment. It is all a question of the magnitude of the assimilation, or conversely of the limitation placed on being smothered by the entwining tentacles of dominant institutions of justice at work. Levels of incorporation may be part and parcel of all attempts to burst the sphere of

---

1 In Harvie and Matthew (2000: 5); emphasis added.

presently dominant justice, to pierce its encompassing meaning horizons in order to calculate justice anew. We are, after all, locally produced subjects who face our times temporally, address what is to come as a future, or as promises fashioned using significations that themselves trace – are constitutive of us and our – present meaning constellations.

With this in mind, the work of restorative justice and its governmentalities should not be narrated as a simple merger with criminal justice. Indeed, the promise to work beyond adversarial images of justice is deeply attractive to many. And the spirit that traces so many of the processes deployed in the restorative name bears the promise of an alternative vision of justice aspiring to challenge the punitive, guilt-seeking, violent, pain-inflicting practices of justice calculated around criminal law and philosophies of the *lex talionis*. This aspiration, particularly evident in the informal justice lineage to which Chapter 1 referred, pledged to resist the cascading flows of adversarial criminal justice. There is, to put it another way, a degree of resistance in this call for alternation, even if it predicated itself upon the very concepts it seeks to transcend.

That restorative justice's iridescent aspiration to pursue such alternatives should have dimmed in direct proportion to its exceptionally successful expansion into criminal justice arenas, such that even its leading lights now question their earlier allegiances to a distinctively different, substitute justice[2] should not diminish the tangible resistances exacted from its rise (Fitzpatrick, 1988). That degrees of resistance may now be unnecessarily, if severely, curtailed is not to say that the pursuit is without its resistances, without openings to idioms beyond the courtroom. Indeed, it may well be that working out of restorative justice's *imitor* paradox, one can glimpse renewed possibilities for calculating justice *outside* criminal law's conceptual horizons.

Five implications of the *imitor* paradox

Discussion over the previous five chapters has located the different contours of the *imitor* paradox by which restorative justice

---

2 For example, Zehr notes: 'In my earlier work, I often drew a sharp contrast between the retributive framework of the legal or criminal justice system and a more restorative approach. More recently, however, I have come to believe that this polarization may be somewhat misleading' (2002: 58). He calls for attempts to isolate areas of similarity and collaboration between the two approaches.

advocates simultaneously pledge allegiance to an alternative to criminal justice, invoking different values (traditions) and processes of justice; yet their options rest ultimately upon key aspects of existing criminal justice systems. As we have seen, in all the areas discussed – harm, victims, offenders, community – this paradox is reproduced. In each sphere of its program, restorative advocates claim radically different visions of justice from criminal justice arrangements whilst ultimately deferring to, and relying on, the latter's key assumptions. As noted too, by drastically limiting the meaning of 'alternative' to criminal justice so that it becomes less a matter of replacement and more a question of complementing, restorative advocates are in danger of compromising the popular appeal that legitimated restorative justice as a different approach in the first place. Let us here turn to five important implications of sustaining this paradox within restorative justice governmentalities under these headings:

- political appeal;
- the impossible structure of restorative justice;
- restorative justice's parasitic identity;
- recalibrating justice ethically; and
- promises of justice to come.

Political appeal

One of the most immediate implications of the paradox within restorative justice governmentalities has to do with the political advantages of clinging to potentially opposing conceptual ideas in current horizons. Perhaps one of the most important reasons for restorative justice's dramatic rise of late has to do with its ability to appeal simultaneously to differing interests. On the one hand, it appeals to people of various shades of contemporary political opinion by claiming to provide a radical alternative to the state's criminal justice system. This assertion is appealing to those on the left because of deep-seated concerns about the capitalist state's ability to yield any just institutions. It simultaneously appeals to 'libertine' politicians on the right because of their neo-liberal calls to roll back the state and enable the privatisation/deregulation of as many welfare state functions as possible. Furthermore, by claiming to complement existing criminal justice institutions, restorative governmentalities appeal to social democrats in search of democratic enhancements of existing state institutions. At the same time, the quest to complement criminal justice arrangements with potentially cost-saving measures appeals to politicians looking for ways to show that they are doing something valuable about a seemingly intractable 'crime problem', with maximum administrative efficiency and minimal cost. It also appeases concerns about the potential for dissent generated by radical alternative propositions to the existing status quo.

Consequently, the *imitor* paradox renders restorative justice attractive to diverse groups, spreading its appeal broadly across the political spectrum. What is yielded in analytic integrity, conceptual clarity and the ethical commitment to an alternative is gained in popular political appeal and the ability to install restorative processes widely within existing arrangements. There is thus much political mileage to be gained from maintaining the paradox and ensuring that its opposing poles are sustained. It should also allude to some costs of maintaining the paradox. For one, as noted, it disallows critical questioning which moves beyond the assumptive universes that sustain both restorative and criminal justice governmentalities. In essence, this sacrifice has turned proponents away from their initial ethical motivations and the quest for alternatives to purportedly flawed criminal justice values, traditions and governmental practices. The restorative promise to provide a vastly different way of conceptualising justice has, in effect, been traduced by sustaining a paradox that enables political accommodations to the current status quo. In the process, the identity of restorative justice as a discrete regulatory practice is blurred, and increasingly is incorporated into its supposed opposite. As such, we now confront a residual, complementary governmentality that serves the very criminal justice its rationales and processes were meant to replace.

The impossible structure of restorative justice

The paradoxical ways in which restorative governmentalities are framed and deployed have generated an identity defined in relation to the justice institutions it claims to oppose. It exists by virtue of claims to simultaneously exceed *and* remain within the terms of criminal justice. It is both inside and outside, friend and foe, dependent and independent, of criminal justice. But these polar terms give a sense of schism at the heart of the identity that is both this and not this, that and not that, at the same time. As a result, there is a profound impossibility at the heart of the identity; an identity fissured around a breach that pulls it in two opposing directions.

Restorative justice is thus impossible. Its quest to exceed criminal justice demands that it does so with a requisite *ecstasis*, a requisite moving beyond the stasis of present legally calculated horizons of justice. However, were it to do that, then restorative justice might have to jettison its defining governmental edifice that revolves around notions like crime, offender, victim, and other stanchions of criminal jurisprudence. On the other hand, if it clings to the latter, then it must betray the quest to exceed criminal justice calculations. This is an impossible bind that paradoxically enables something like the restorative governmentalities we have described to emerge. Restorative justice is thus structured around the impossible. Ironically, the impossible structure of restorative justice makes possible something like the governmental logic, experience and techniques that we have encountered. In this respect, the impossible lies at the very heart of restorative justice; it is the very foundation upon which the paradoxical identity of restorative justice has over the past few decades been built.

It is important to note a point of clarification. Saying that restorative justice is structured on impossible grounds is not to say that it is impossible in the sense that it does not, or cannot, exist. Rather, it is to say that the governmentality's current identity has been made possible precisely because of an impossible, paradoxical trace that lurks as a constitutive dimension of its emergence. We are not dealing with, say, a timeless, stable, fixed, necessary, absolute or independent identity (there is no such thing). Restorative justice is instead contingently constituted on the basis of an impossible aporia that highlights the more or less arbitrary historical performances that bring sequences of sometimes quite disparate events to coalesce around the name 'restorative justice'. If nothing else, I take this realisation to emphasise the non-absolute, non-necessary, undetermined, finite and transient arrival of restorative justice governmentalities. Their impossible structure betokens the finitude of restorative justice calculations, and the brazenly laudable attempts to exceed the identity of criminal justice.

Restorative justice's parasitic identity

If the structure of impossibility challenges the sense of restorative justice as a necessary, singular identity, the *imitor* paradox compromises any quest for those aspiring to exceed criminal justice to arrive as a fully autonomous identity. However, it may be that restorative justice's close attachments to criminal justice institutions have contingently narrowed its alternative claims to justice; during the course of its relatively short history, restorative justice has made itself vitally dependent upon criminal justice assumptions and categories to identify itself (for example, on the basis of 'crime', 'victim', 'offender', etc). As such, and as Braithwaite notes:

> Restorative justice is most commonly defined by what it is an alternative to. Juvenile justice, for example, is seen as seesawing back and forth during the past century between justice and a welfare model, between retribution and rehabilitation. Restorative justice is touted as a long-overdue third model or a new 'lens' ... a way of hopping off the see-saw ... (2002: 10).

The inability to define restorative justice absolutely may not be so much a failure as a feature of language. As Derrida (1976, 1995) notes, signs always defer to other signs for meaning, leaving us without the ability to close off language absolutely and underscoring its dynamic contingency. The meaning of any identity may well then rely constitutively on its absence, on systems of *'différance'* (with the 'a') through which signs refer to others to create a 'presence', a being. However brief and oversimplified these statements might be, they at least highlight this point: there are ontological consequences produced by given systems of differance, by the ways in which signs defer to one another in a given discourse. The way in which signs are assembled to generate meaning constellations is deeply consequential for how we come to live our lives.

However, this means that so long as restorative justice defines itself through systems of differance that defer to basic criminal justice assumptions, thereby entrenching its dependence on the latter, the degree to which it is able to exceed such assumptions is unduly truncated. This suggests again that an alternative calculation of justice need not position itself as a servant of state criminal justice decrees.

By seeking to complement criminal justice, and deferring to fundamental criminal justice assumptions for its being, restorative justice renders itself *parasitic* upon existing criminal justice arrangements (see Woolford and Ratner, 2003). This has profound ramifications for the identity (and existence) of restorative justice, betraying a deep-seated ontological dependence on current criminal justice arrangements. There may well be reciprocal dependencies, but criminal justice governmentalities appeal to a far wider system of differance, and so maintain a broader identity formation (eg, by engaging jurisprudence, criminology, penology, criminal justice, law, sociology, political science, etc). In restricting restorative initiatives to being relevant, complementary, and so on, restorative justice has allowed its calculations to depend constitutively upon its supposed opposite.

Furthermore, an alternative that defines itself in relation to, and uses the concepts of, the very approach it seeks to replace is either a parasitic or a non-distinct venture. So long as restorative justice defines itself as a complement to criminal justice, it cannot exist without the latter. It certainly cannot replace criminal justice, for that would imply an independent identity capable of accomplishing such a replacement. Were it actually to overcome criminal justice, restorative justice would lose the discursive anchor against which it has defined itself, to which its key linguistic concepts defer. Without criminal justice, in short, the self-defined complement would lose its meaning – quite literally, its structure of differance would disappear. Its systems of deferring would be lost, rendering the current 'restorative justice' governmentalities meaningless. In other words, one might say that a governmentality which defines itself as an appended alternative would have no meaning whatsoever without the anchoring concepts that it serves.

Restorative justice as an alternative in this sense is unattainable because it constitutes its identity largely by deferring to the very (criminal justice) institutions it seeks to replace, reform, alter, etc. Were those institutions to change, a goal many proponents actively pursue, restorative justice would be left without the founding auspices of its current identity, without traces for its sign constellations to defer. By building its identity on not being criminal justice, restorative proponents have left themselves little room for autochthonous enunciation. Any claim to an identity in excess of the state's criminal justice is paradoxically made by deferring to its underlying assumptions, predicating restorative justice upon the very thing that it is supposed to alter. Ironically, this again confirms that the quest for a restorative justice as an independent alternative to criminal justice is impossible, and it is that very impossibility which sustains the possibility of restorative governmentalities as 'complementary alternative' to existing criminal justice structures.

However, were restorative significations to erect themselves in relation to sign constellations beyond criminal justice system governmentalities, one could expect a very different vision of justice to emerge. The claim to being an alternative would also resound to a far larger extent beyond, in excess of, existing structures. So, the distinction to bear in mind is not that of restorative versus criminal justice; instead it is restorative and criminal justice versus a justice that is yet to arrive. That is, if the aim is to seek ways of enunciating alternatives to existing rationales and practices of governing in the name of justice, then it is perhaps best to situate criminal and restorative justice not in opposition, but as similar sorts of calculations of justice. It is not that justice is calculated either as restorative restitution or criminal retribution, but rather that together these interlocking paradigms form one pole of what potentially could be opposed to a new horizon of justice with very different concepts and ideas. The quest would, no doubt, involve notions of justice beyond both restorative and criminal governmentalities.

This recognition is acknowledged by restorative justice literatures where the sharp divisions between restorative justice's victim-centred, problem-resolution approach and the state's (alleged) retributive focus on punishing guilty offenders is challenged. Several commentators, for example, note that punishment is by no means absent from restorative processes (Daly, 2003b: 363–66).[3] Even Braithwaite's famous 'reintegrative shaming', while clearly meant as a corrective to destructive (non-

---

3 Daly argues thus: 'Reverence for and romanticization of an indigenous past slide over practices that the modern "civilized" western mind would object to, such as the variety of harsh physical (bodily) punishments and banishment. At the same time, the modern western mind may not be able to grasp how certain "harsh punishments" have been sensible within the terms of a particular culture' (Daly, 2003b: 367). She notes further: 'Is it appropriate to refer to all of these practices as "restorative"? No, I think not. What do these practices in fact have in common? What is gained, and more importantly, what is lost by this homogenizing move?' (Daly, 2003b: 368).

integrative) punishments, necessarily entails degrees of punishment.[4] The basic point of the debate is this: despite claims to the contrary, retribution and punishment are not absent from restorative control horizons.[5] In addition, both restorative and criminal justice sometimes defer to medical model notions of healing when approaching 'crime'.[6] Furthermore, it is not at all clear that restorative and restitutive practices are absent from criminal law (Woolford and Ratner, 2003; Walgrave, 1999). Zehr (2003) acknowledges the significance of civil law and notes that

---

4 Taking this further, Levrant *et al* show just how far coercion and 'getting tough' mentalities are integrated into restorative justice practices; without due process safeguards, they worry that restorative justice has the potential to 'increase the punitiveness of the social control imposed on offenders' (1999: 371). Furthermore, although naked vengeance may offend restorative values, a degree of contrition for 'crimes' committed, often with punitive intent, is expected of participants in conferences. On a related tack, Duff (2002) argues that rehabilitative forms of punishment *should* be part of any restorative efforts.

5 Likewise, and by contrast, one may challenge the view that criminal law is only – or even primarily – retributive, devoid of restorative elements. In many ways, this is a view of criminal law overly influenced by classical criminological perspectives. No doubt, Beccaria's (1963) age-old classical tenets remain relevant to some degree in neo-classical revivals and current 'get tough on crime' ethos. However, the residual influence of equally influential positivist criminological approaches remains evident in contemporary criminal justice systems. One could, for example, refer to the focus on rehabilitation, correctionalist, and disciplinary responses to crime (Pfohl, 1994; Foucault, 1977). Drawing on medical models, positivist criminologists view crime as a legal reflection of prior 'norms'; 'criminals' commit crime because of biological, genetic or psychological traits. It is worth noting that for positivists the appropriate response to crime is to diagnose and 'treat', or set about healing, underlying pathologies. Such healing language is certainly related to talk of healing so firmly entrenched within restorative discourses. Hence, one may see why Bazemore and O'Brien (2002) would think it possible to find a 'restorative model of rehabilitation'. Finally, restorative processes are not devoid of rules and expectations, just as criminal justice systems are not devoid of significant degrees of discretion. See Gelsthorpe and Padfield (2003) and Ashworth (1998).

6 Notwithstanding Braithwaite (2002: 3) and Johnstone's (2002: 5) astute warnings about seeing restoration as a new version of rehabilitation.

fines provide a model for restitutive justice.[7] The point echoed through all of these debates is the homologous overlaps between restorative and criminal justice.

If restorative justice is parasitically built on the foundations of already existing criminal responses to crime, can it nonetheless establish a unique niche? Perhaps there is a trade-off between legitimating restorative justice as a substitute for failing criminal justice initiatives and the quest to serve that system. Being relevant to existing governmental contexts may compromise the spirit of trying to develop an alternative that redresses key problems with existing criminal justice approaches. Remaining relevant and calculating justice anew is an impossible trade-off, but it may also suggest the possibility of recalibrating justice in a rather different way – as always a promise yet to come.

Recalibrating justice ethically

Within restorative governmentalities, we are implored to imagine a new paradigm of justice, a new way of dealing with crime. However, when justice is approached through ethical languages within restorative governmentalities, it is often seen through particular theological lenses (eg, Consedine, 1995; Zehr, 1990). These lenses have helped to frame restorative justice as a value and set of processes, such as its role in 'healing the harm' of crime. In addition, problem-solving, future-directed restorative practices defer to a version of the medical model and the very criminal justice assumptions they claim to replace. Restorative governmentalities here relocate discussions of justice outside moral and ethical languages. This all too often leads proponents to embrace technicist, administrative and even managerial reasons to explain the intrinsic value of restorative justice as something to pursue. In turn, the *imitor* paradox – despite calls to

---

7 Johnstone too notes that: '… it is highly likely that many criminalisable events are already being interpreted and handled within a restorative justice framework, ie they are handled with the state's involvement and with an emphasis on recompense and contrition rather than punitive suffering. It is indeed likely that, in social practice, restorative justice is more the norm, and stayed punitive justice the exception' (2002: 59). In a related way, one could argue that criminal justice systems are mostly focused on restitution when dealing with first-time offenders (hence the emphasis, for example, on diversion and community service programs). All such points make clear that the restitutive-retributive distinction alleged by many restorative justice proponents is much less clear than one might take from many accounts.

envisage restorative justice as requiring a change of moral paradigms – may be read as signalling a virtual retreat from any ethical meaning horizons.

Doubtless, there would be a profit to recovering an ethical language that addresses justice not as an ontological (existing) absolute entity that is manifest through institutions declaring themselves as just. The pursuit of discourses that exceed both restorative and dominant legal frameworks of justice might approach the idea of justice, not as an ontology which declares what is essential to, or absolutely proper for, justice; instead, it might evoke ethical precepts to grapple with the undetermined, infinite and never fully present moments in which the name of justice is called upon to deliver subjects from one sort of being to another. We should recall that ethics is possible precisely when there are undetermined, inessential choices at stake. Where life is fully determined, there is no choice, and so no ethics. The language of ethics becomes possible because of the radical undecidability of given moments.

So, instead of gathering concepts to 'discover' justice as ontology with fixed, essential characteristics, one could imagine justice as a never closed, never fully calculable, open and infinite idea that promises new ways to be with others. Derrida (1992) elaborates upon such an open-ended notion of justice.[8] Although this is not the place to pursue his thought in any detail, suffice to note that he begins with a seemingly curious, but profoundly significant, statement: 'There is no such thing as justice.' It does not exist as such. When someone declares 'I am just', or 'this process is just', they thereby mistake justice for an ontology, as something which exists, and so lose sight of its ethical, undecidable, never fully present meaning horizons. Justice is never an absolute entity, a reality or even a definable ideal to which our institutions might strive. Justice instead implies:

> non-gathering, dissociation, heterogeneity, non-identity with itself, endless inadequation, infinite transcendence. That is why the call to justice is never, never fully answered. That is why no one can say 'I am just'. If someone tells you 'I am just', you can be sure that he or she is wrong, because being just is not a matter of theoretical determination (Derrida, 1997: 17).

If anything, justice is an incalculable, non-definable idea that forever calls us from the mists of what is to arrive. Related to

---

8   See also Lyotard and Thébaud (1985) and Pavlich (1996a: Chapter 2).

Kant's transcendental ideas, it is always projected beyond as an infinite promise that can never finitely arrive. Justice emerges as an incalculable promise, but nevertheless one that requires calculations to be made in its name; law and restorative justice are two such calculations, but neither is ever entirely just, for justice always extends beyond a specific reckoning.

It is thus important to approach local calculations of justice with a sense of disquiet, remaining vigilant to their inevitable dangers and open to other possible computations. This underscores the importance of opening up to the arrival of unexpected events, ideas, and thereby preventing any image of justice from declaring itself as necessary, or as intrinsically better than any other. In the uneasy comforts of such decrees resides a spectre of totalitarian formations. So, one may insist upon a primary responsibility to what lies outside, what is other to, a given calculation of the just. This ethical formulation of justice implies a sense of justice that welcomes alterity, and never portrays the present as necessary; any given present is always constituted by its connection with what is absent. It also understands justice to constantly recalculate the borders of present limit formations.

With this different ethical horizon, it becomes possible to recalibrate justice in precepts that exceed restorative and criminal justice computations. Although it would reverse the spirit of the foregoing to declare with certainty what any specific calibration ought – necessarily – to be, one could nevertheless attend to another more relevant matter: what can one learn from the *imitor* paradox by way of calculating justice without deferring to key criminal justice precepts?

Just promises, anew?

As we have seen, the *imitor* paradox revolves around at least four key assumptions within criminal justice horizons: *crime, victim, offender* and *community*. These bind the governmentality to the everyday concepts of an ethos. But if the aim is to formulate calculations in excess of current justice horizons, it may be useful to work a way through the impossibilities of the *imitor* paradox, to erect sign constellations in excess of its conceptual foundations. In an ethos so centrally defined through the above categories, from its culture to everyday practice, the task may appear to some as laughably absurd. Can justice really be imagined without crime, victims, offenders or communities?

However, it is precisely the silent crevasses of impossibility that allegations of absurdity mask, the cleaving transition from one meaning constellation to another, which is raised as a question here. For, not quite three centuries ago, let us recall, the thought that such precepts would ordain themselves as exclusive organisers of the just might have raised similarly incredulous guffaws. Extending the laughter of the ages, it may be poignant to allude to potential calculations of an ecstatic aspiration to justice, without deferring centrally to such founding concepts. Any attempt to puncture pervasive meaning horizons of restorative and criminal justice, using new frameworks to calculate the promise of justice differently, should be mindful of not replicating the *imitor* paradox *as far as possible*.

By way of an opening to other horizons, the following paragraphs might be read as cautionary remarks about the kind of justice that could be at stake. For example, Chapters 2–5 allude to the central place that legal definitions of crime play in criminal justice calculations and – even if by default – restorative governmentalities. One might ponder the implications for restorative justice as an alternative practice were its proponents to follow through with their critiques of crime, and perhaps even reject legal formulations of crime as the basis of the harms wrested upon victims, offenders and communities. What effects would developing calculations of justice without crime have on the processes used to deploy an alternative justice?

The very prospect is not quite as outlandish as those ensconced in cultures of crime may take it to be; a battery of critical criminologists have long argued that definitions of what constitutes a crime are always the fluid outcomes of socio-political struggles, as opposed to self-evident reflections of a pre-defined 'reality'.[9] From this vantage, the political processes that define 'crime', that bring the concept into being, are as consequential as the processes that lead to the creation of specific criminal identities in local contexts. To accept these human decisions as fundamental or primordial categories is itself a political decision; moreover, it is one made in favour of, and as a support for, the current legal status quo.

What might such calculations of justice entail? Of course, there are many possible variants – for example, one might evoke

---

9   See Milovanovic (2002), Pavlich (2001), Christie (2000), Taylor (1999) and generally Hinch (1994).

diverse experiences of *injustice* (as opposed to crime) as the most immediate and basic call to justice. Calculations of justice would be evoked when an injustice is experienced; it is then that subjects – 'singularly plural, or plurally singular' (Nancy, 2000) – do often turn to the idea of justice in search of new ways to be with others. Thus, one might frame calculations of justice directly around, say, immediate experiences of injustice as defined in local contexts. No doubt, the spectre of vigilantism appears though this enunciation, not unlike restorative justice (see Roche, 2003), occasioning the need for further calibrations of how to address these logically and procedurally. This makes clear that responding to locally framed injustice could be accomplished in all sorts of ways, and through diverse institutions (Pavlich, 2000). This need not exclude either criminal or restorative justice processes in all instances, but it would radically limit the inordinate privilege that both have managed to secure in contemporary justice terrains. The aim would be to seek calculations of justice that do not take for granted, or accept in large measure,[10] legal formulations of crime as the necessary mobilising event for justice. This sort of calculation would also emphasise the need to develop an apposite politics of crime, harm and injustice – the terms of which would have to be developed in far more detail.

Additionally, one might consider the prospect of resisting an ethos that emphasises individual victim and offender identities in its calibrations of justice. As Chapter 3 indicated, the idea of empowering victims of crime *as individual victims* may be tenable in particular cases. However, if one's aim is to transcend the victim identity, to enable those who have been disabled by injustice, is the obligation to assume an individual victim identity always most apposite? As noted too, to what extent is it possible to empower a disempowered – even if temporarily so – identity? What about the political resources and possibilities that might be available to collective consolidations, for those who suffer as a consequence of the interactive effects of broader political envelopes? Very often conflicts, or injustices at local or broader levels, allow – even if for fleeting moments – almost invisible power formations to surface. Wresting the embedded power formations out of their shelters, enabling subject resistance to

---

10 Of course, merely referring to crime legitimates its standing to some degree but, by rendering it marginal to a calculation, the balance of signing forces is shifted.

respond in whatever guise is politically feasible in context, and not obliging all to accept individual victim identities, implies a calculation of justice in excess of that which pervades current legal horizons.

Similarly, and as Chapter 4 clarified, there may be some purchase in not, as a matter of course, accepting legal definitions of the guilty offender. In some cases, it may well be appropriate to generate the offender identity, perhaps in the relatively smaller proportion of violent injustices. Yet there should never be complete closure around the political environments that define offenders, or indeed isolate perpetrators of injustice. From the moment of accusation, from the moment cultural resources mobilise rituals that decide who are strangers in their midst, who is to be designated a perpetrator of harm, who is to make amends, one might well seek to develop an open politics which enables a dialogue to direct itself back to the means of accusation, as well as the basis upon which an accusation is made. Tying accusation to promises of justice is precisely the sort of politics that is at stake here.

On top of this, one might work out of the *imitor* paradox depicted in Chapter 5 to worry about calculating justice with reference to a closed community deployed in large measure by state formations, or whose strength is tied to the active participation of (individual) crime victim and offender identities. Seeking to surpass the totalitarian dangers associated with, or at least not avoided by, such closure, one might focus on the open-ended spirit of spontaneous mutual solidarity that traces many different quests for community. One problem is how this spirit is betrayed by approaching the community as something essentially fixed, definable and so potentially closed.

The question 'what is community?' implies (ironically, given the open appearance of the question) the prior existence of community and reduces the ethical question of how we *could* be with others to a question of ontological necessity (ie, how, given our human nature, we *must* live with one another). Eschewing this ontological question, a different calculation of justice could instead redraft a response to injustice by asking how it could be possible to exist thus, and seeking new ways to be with others. This ethical meaning horizon could, perhaps, align with quests for a community that never is, that never arrives (eg, Nancy, 1991; Agamben, 1993), but I am more inclined to trace the spirit though other allegorical images – such as Derrida's concept of hospitality (Pavlich, 2004, 2002b). Regardless, the calculation of justice may be tied to experiences of injustice within a given collective formation, and the ethical quest to seek styles of living in ways not attached to perceived injustices, to face up to the constitutive responsibility of being differently with others.

Even this hesitant attempt at opening to a different promise of justice begins with its own paradoxical attachments to past legacies and concepts. Perhaps this is inevitable to some degree when framing something new, when seeking new institutions. Derrida put the matter thus:

> The paradox in the instituting moment of an institution is that, at the same time that it starts something new, it also continues something, is true to the memory of the past, to a heritage, to something we receive from the past, from our predecessors, from the culture. If an institution is to be an institution, it must to some extent break with the past, keep the memory of the past, while incorporating something absolutely new (Derrida, 1997: 6).

If this book has been an avid attempt to open up to justice anew, it is equally an attempt to be true to a memory of the past, to promises of justice that beckon ceaseless beyond the horizons of time. One could begin with the promise of another existence, traced by an obdurate glow of just promises that exceed what we have come to be.

Bibliography

Abel, Richard L (ed), 1982, *The Politics of Informal Justice*, New York: Academic Press

Achilles, Mary and Zehr, Howard, 2001, 'Restorative Justice for Crime Victims: The Promise, the Challenge', in Bazemore, Gordon and Schiff, Mara (eds), *Restorative Community Justice: Repairing Harm and Transforming Communities*, Cincinnati, OH: Anderson, pp 87–100

Acorn, Annalise E, 2004, *Compulsory Compassion: A Critique of Restorative Justice*, Vancouver: UBC Press

Agamben, Giorgio, 1993, *The Coming Community*, Minneapolis, MN: University of Minnesota Press

Akester, Kate, 2002, 'Restorative Justice, Victims' Rights and the Future', *Legal Action Group Policy*, January: 1–4

Allard, Pierre and Northey, Wayne, 2003, 'Christianity: The Rediscovery of Restorative Justice', in Johnstone, Gerry (ed), *A Restorative Justice Reader: Texts, Sources, Context*, Cullompton: Willan, pp 158–70

Amit, Vered (ed), 2002, *Realizing Community: Concepts, Social Relationships and Sentiments*, London: Routledge

Ashworth, Andrew, 1993, 'Some Doubts About Restorative Justice', *Criminal Law Forum* 4: 277–99

Ashworth, Andrew, 1998, *The Criminal Process*, Oxford: OUP

Ashworth, Andrew, 2003a, 'Is Restorative Justice the Way Forward for Criminal Justice?', in McLaughlin, Eugene, Fergusson, Ross, Hughes, Gordon and Westmarland, Louise (eds), *Restorative Justice: Critical Issues*, London: Sage (Open University), pp 164–81

Ashworth, Andrew, 2003b, 'Responsibilities, Rights and Restorative Justice', in Johnstone, Gerry (ed), *A Restorative Justice Reader: Texts, Sources, Context*, Cullompton: Willan, pp 426–37

Auerbach, Jerold S, 1983, *Justice without Law?*, New York: OUP

Ayto, John, 1990, *Dictionary of Word Origins*, London: Bloomsbury

Barnett, Randy, 2003, 'Restitution: A New Paradigm of Criminal Justice', in Johnstone, Gerry (ed), *A Restorative Justice Reader: Texts, Sources, Context*, Cullompton: Willan, pp 46–56

Barton, Charles KB, 2003, *Restorative Justice: The Empowerment Model*, Sydney: Hawkins

Bauman, Zygmunt, 1992, *Intimations of Postmodernity*, London: Routledge

Bauman, Zygmunt, 1994, *Alone Again: Ethics After Certainty*, London: Demos

Bauman, Zygmunt, 1997, *Postmodernity and its Discontents*, Cambridge: Polity

Bauman, Zygmunt, 2001, *Community: Seeking Safety in an Insecure World*, Cambridge: Polity

Bazemore, Gordon, 1998, 'Restorative Justice and Earned Redemption: Communities, Victims, and Offender Reintegration', *American Behavioral Scientist* 41: 768–813

Bazemore, Gordon and Griffiths, Curt, 2003, 'Conferences, Circles, Boards and Mediations: The New Wave of Community Justice Decision Making', in McLaughlin, Eugene, Fergusson, Ross, Hughes, Gordon and Westmarland, Louise (eds), *Restorative Justice: Critical Issues*, London: Sage (Open University), pp 73–84

Bazemore, Gordon and McLeod, Colleen, 2002, 'Restorative Justice and the Future of Diversion and Informal Social Control', in Weitekamp, Elmar and Kerner, Hans-Jürgen (eds), *Restorative Justice: Theoretical Foundations*, Cullompton: Willan, pp 111–42

Bazemore, Gordon and O'Brien, Sandra, 2002, 'The Quest for a Restorative Model of Rehabilitation', in Walgrave, Lode (ed), *Restorative Justice and the Law*, Cullompton: Willan, pp 31–67

Bazemore, Gordon, Pranis, Kay and Umbreit, Mark, 1997, *Balanced and Restorative Justice for Juveniles: A Framework for Juvenile Justice in the 21st Century*, Washington, DC: Office of Juvenile Justice and Delinquency Prevention

Bazemore, Gordon and Schiff, Mara (eds), 2001, *Restorative Community Justice: Repairing Harm and Transforming Communities*, Cincinnati, OH: Anderson

Bazemore, Gordon and Taylor, Curt, 1997, 'Conferences, Circles, Boards and Mediations: The "New Wave" of Community Justice Decisionmaking', *Federal Probation* 61: 25–37

Bazemore, Gordon and Umbreit, Mark, 1995, 'Rethinking the Sanctioning Function in Juvenile Court: Retributive or Restorative Responses to Youth Crime', *Crime and Delinquency* 41: 296–316

Bazemore, Gordon and Umbreit, Mark, 1999, *Conferences, Circles, Boards and Mediations: Restorative Justice and Citizen Involvement in the Response to Youth Crime*, St Paul, MN: University of Minnesota, Center for Restorative Justice and Mediation

Bazemore, Gordon and Umbreit, Mark, 2003, 'A Comparison of Four Restorative Conferencing Models', in Johnstone, Gerry (ed), *A Restorative Justice Reader: Texts, Sources, Context*, Cullompton: Willan, pp 225–44

Bazemore, Gordon and Walgrave, Lode, 1999, *Restorative Juvenile Justice: Repairing the Harm of Youth Crime*, Monsey, NY: Criminal Justice Press

Beccaria, Cesare, 1963, *On Crimes and Punishments*, Indianapolis, IN: Bobbs-Merrill

Bentham, Jeremy, 1890, *Theory of Legislation*, London: Truber and Co

Bohannan, Paul, 1957, *Justice and Judgment Amongst the Tiv*, Oxford: OUP

Bonta, James, Wallace-Capretta, Suzanne and Rooney, Jennifer, 1998, *Restorative Justice: An Evaluation of the Restorative Resolutions Project*, Ottawa: Solicitor General Canada

Bottoms, Anthony, 2003, 'Some Sociological Reflections on Restorative Justice', in von Hirsch, Andrew, Roberts, Julian and Bottoms, Anthony (eds), *Restorative Justice and Criminal Justice: Competing or Reconcilable Paradigms*, Oxford: Hart, pp 79–114

Braithwaite, John, 1989, *Crime, Shame and Reintegration*, Cambridge: CUP

Braithwaite, John, 1998, 'Restorative Justice', in Tonry, Michael (ed), *The Handbook of Crime and Punishment*, New York: OUP

Braithwaite, John, 1999, 'Restorative Justice: Assessing Optimistic and Pessimistic Accounts', *Crime and Justice* 25: 1–127

Braithwaite, John, 2000a, *Regulation, Crime, Freedom*, Burlington, VT: Ashgate/Dartmouth

Braithwaite, John, 2000b, 'Repentance Rituals and Restorative Justice', *Journal of Political Philosophy* 8: 115–32

Braithwaite, John, 2002, *Restorative Justice and Responsive Regulation*, Oxford: OUP

Braithwaite, John, 2003a, 'Restorative Justice and Social Justice', in McLaughlin, Eugene, Fergusson, Ross, Hughes, Gordon and Westmarland, Louise (eds), *Restorative Justice: Critical Issues*, London: Sage (Open University), pp 157–63

Braithwaite, John, 2003b, 'Principles of Restorative Justice', in von Hirsch, Andrew, Roberts, Julian and Bottoms, Anthony (eds), *Restorative Justice and Criminal Justice: Competing or Reconcilable Paradigms*, Oxford: Hart, pp 1–20

Braithwaite, John and Mugford, Stephen, 1994, 'Conditions of Successful Reintegration Ceremonies: Dealing with Juvenile Offenders', *British Journal of Criminology* 34: 139–71

Braithwaite, John and Roach, Declan, 2001, 'Responsibility and Restorative Justice', in Bazemore, Gordon and Schiff, Mara (eds), *Restorative Community Justice: Repairing Harm and Transforming Communities*, Cincinnati, OH: Anderson, pp 63–84

British Columbia Ministry of Attorney General, 1998, *A Restorative Justice Framework: British Columbia Justice Reform*, Victoria: British Columbia Ministry of Attorney General

Brown, BJ and McElrea, FWM, 1993, *The Youth Court in New Zealand: A New Model of Justice*, Auckland: Legal Research Foundation

Burchell, Graham, 1991, 'Peculiar Interests: Civil Society and Governing "the System of Natural Liberty"', in Burchell, Graham, Gordon, Colin and Miller, Peter (eds), *The Foucault Effect: Studies in Governmentality*, Chicago, IL: University of Chicago Press

Bush, Robert and Folger, Joseph, 1994, *The Promise of Mediation: Responding to Conflict through Empowerment*, San Francisco, CA: Jossey-Bass

Canada, Law Commission of, 2003, *Transforming Relationships through Participatory Justice*, Ottawa: Minister of Public Works

Carson, WG, 2004a, 'Is Communalism Dead? Reflections on the Present and Future Practice of Crime Prevention (Part 1)', *Australian and New Zealand Journal of Criminology* 37: 1–21

Carson, WG, 2004b, 'Is Communalism Dead? Reflections on the Present and Future Practice of Crime Prevention (Part 2)', *Australian and New Zealand Journal of Criminology* 37: 192–210

Christie, Nils, 1977, 'Conflict as Property', *British Journal of Criminology* 17: 1–5

Christie, Nils, 2000, *Crime Control as Industry: Towards Gulags, Western Style*, New York: Routledge

Clear, Todd R and Karp, David, 2000, 'Toward the Ideal of Community Justice', *National Institute of Justice Journal*, October: 20–28

Clear, Todd R and Karp, David, 2002, *What Is Community Justice? Case Studies of Restorative Justice and Community Supervision*, Thousand Oaks, CA: Sage

Cohen, Anthony, 2002, 'Epilogue', in Amit, Vered (ed), *Realizing Community: Concepts, Social Relationships and Sentiments*, London: Routledge, p 173

Cohen, Stanley, 1985, *Visions of Social Control: Crime, Punishment, and Classification*, Oxford: Polity

Cohen, Stanley, 2001, *States of Denial: Knowing About Atrocities and Suffering*, Malden, MA: Polity

Colson, Charles W, 2001, *Justice That Restores*, Wheaton, IL: Tyndale House

Consedine, Jim, 1995, *Restorative Justice: Healing the Effects of Crime*, Lyttleton, NZ: Ploughshares

Consedine, Jim and Bowen, Helen, 1999, *Restorative Justice: Contemporary Themes and Practice*, Lyttleton, NZ: Ploughshares

Cooley, Dennis, 1999, *From Restorative Justice to Transformative Justice: Discussion Paper*, Ottawa: Law Commission of Canada

Corlett, William, 1989, *Community Without Unity: A Politics of Derridian Extravagance*, Durham, NC: Duke UP

Cragg, Wesley, 1992, *The Practice of Punishment: Towards a Theory of Restorative Justice*, London: Routledge

Crawford, Adam, 1998, 'Community Safety and the Quest for Security: Holding Back the Dynamics of Social Exclusion', *Policy Studies* 19: 237–53

Crawford, Adam, 2002, 'The State, Community and Restorative Justice: Heresy, Nostalgia and Butterfly Collecting', in Walgrave, Lode (ed), *Restorative Justice and the Law*, Cullompton: Willan, pp 101–29

Crawford, Adam and Clear, Todd, 2003, 'Community Justice: Transforming Communities through Restorative Justice', in McLaughlin, Eugene, Fergusson, Ross, Hughes, Gordon and Westmarland, Louise (eds), *Restorative Justice: Critical Issues*, London: Sage (Open University), pp 215–29

Crawford, Adam and Newburn, Tim, 2003, *Youth Offending and Restorative Justice: Implementing Reform in Youth Justice*, Cullompton: Willan

Critchley, Simon, 1992, *The Ethics of Deconstruction: Derrida and Levinas*, Oxford: Blackwell

Critchley, Simon, 1999, *Ethics, Politics and Subjectivity*, London: Verso

Cullen, Francis T and Gilbert, Karen E, 1982, *Reaffirming Rehabilitation*, Cincinnati, OH: Anderson

Cunneen, Chris, 2002, 'Restorative Justice and the Politics of Belonging', in Weitekamp, Elmar and Kerner, Hans-Jürgen (eds), *Restorative Justice: Theoretical Foundations*, Cullompton: Willan, pp 32–49

Cunneen, Chris, 2004, 'What are the Implications of Restorative Justice's Use of Indigenous Traditions?', in Zehr, Howard and Toews, Barb (eds), *Critical Issues in Restorative Justice*, New York: Criminal Justice Press, pp 341–50

Daly, Kathleen, 2000, 'Revisiting the Relationship between Retributive and Restorative Justice', in Strang, Heather and Braithwaite, John (eds), *Restorative Justice: From Philosophy to Practice*, Dartmouth: Ashgate, pp 33–54

Daly, Kathleen, 2003a, 'Mind the Gap: Restorative Justice in Theory and Practice', in von Hirsch, Andrew, Roberts, Julian and Bottoms, Anthony (eds), *Restorative Justice and Criminal Justice: Competing or Reconcilable Paradigms*, Oxford: Hart, pp 219–36

Daly, Kathleen, 2003b, 'Restorative Justice: The Real Story', in Johnstone, Gerry (ed), *A Restorative Justice Reader*, Cullompton: Willan, pp 361–72

Daniels, Roger, 2003, *An Age of Apology?*, Kingston, Ont: Kashtan

Danzig, Richard, 1973, 'Towards the Creation of a Complementary, Decentralized System of Criminal Justice', *Stanford Law Review* 26: 1–54

Dean, Mitchell, 1999, *Governmentality: Power and Rule in Modern Society*, London: Sage

Delanty, Gerard, 2003, *Community*, London: Routledge

Derrida, Jacques, 1976, *Of Grammatology*, Baltimore, MD: Johns Hopkins UP

Derrida, Jacques, 1992, 'The Force of Law: The "Mystical Foundation of Authority"', in Cornell, Drucilla, Rosenfeld, Michel, Carlson, David and Benjamin, Neil (eds), *Deconstruction and the Possibility of Justice*, New York: Routledge, p 409

Derrida, Jacques, 1994, *Specters of Marx: The State of the Debt, the Work of Mourning, and the New International*, New York: Routledge

Derrida, Jacques, 1995, *Points ...: Interviews, 1974–1994*, Stanford, CA: Stanford UP

Derrida, Jacques, 1997, *Deconstruction in a Nutshell: A Conversation with Jacques Derrida*, New York: Fordham UP

Derrida, Jacques, 1999, *Adieu to Emmanuel Levinas*, Stanford, CA: Stanford UP

Derrida, Jacques, 2000, 'Hospitality', *Angelaki* 5: 3–18

Derrida, Jacques, 2001, *On Cosmopolitanism and Forgiveness*, London: Routledge

Derrida, Jacques and Dufourmantelle, Anne, 2000, *Of Hospitality*, Stanford: Stanford UP

Dignan, James, 2002, 'Restorative Justice and the Law: The Case for an Integrated Systematic Approach', in Walgrave, Lode (ed), *Restorative Justice and the Law*, Cullompton: Willan, pp 168–90

Dignan, James and Cavadino, Michael, 1996, 'Towards a Framework for Conceptualising and Evaluating Models of Criminal Justice from a Victim's Perspective', *International Review of Victimology* 4: 153–82

Doerner, William G and Lab, Steven P, 1998, *Victimology*, Cincinnati, OH: Anderson

Duff, Antony, 2002, 'Restorative Punishment and Punitive Restoration', in Walgrave, Lode (ed), *Restorative Justice and the Law*, Cullompton: Willan, pp 82–100

Etzioni, Amitai (ed), 1998, *The Essential Communitarian Reader*, Lanham, MD: Rowman & Littlefield

Fisher, Eric, 1975, 'Community Courts: An Alternative to Conventional Adjudication', *American University Law Review* 24: 1253–91

Fitzpatrick, Peter, 1988, 'The Rise and Rise of Informal Justice', in Matthews, Roger (ed), *Informal Justice?*, London: Sage, p 214

Ford Foundation, 1978, *Mediating Social Conflict*, New York: Ford Foundation

Foucault, Michel, 1977, *Discipline and Punish: The Birth of the Prison*, New York: Pantheon

Foucault, Michel, 1980, *Power/Knowledge: Selected Interviews and Other Writings, 1972–1977*, Brighton: Harvester

Foucault, Michel, 1994, *Ethics: Subjectivity and Truth*, New York: The New Press

Frank, Jerome, 1970, *Courts on Trial: Myth and Reality in American Justice*, New York: Atheneum

Furedi, Frank, 2004, *Therapy Culture: Cultivating Vulnerability in an Uncertain Age*, London: Routledge

Furio, Jennifer, 2002, *Restorative Justice*, New York: Algora

Galaway, Burt and Hudson, Joe, 1996, *Restorative Justice: International Perspectives*, Monsey, NY: Criminal Justice Press

Garland, David (ed), 2001, *Mass Imprisonment: Social Causes and Consequences*, London: Sage

Gelsthorpe, Loraine and Padfield, Nicola (eds), 2003, *Exercising Discretion: Decision-Making in the Criminal Justice System and Beyond*, Cullompton: Willan

Gluckman, Max, 1965, *Politics, Law and Ritual Tribal Society*, Oxford: Basil Blackwell

Graef, Roger, 2001, *Why Restorative Justice? Repairing the Harm Caused by Crime*, London: Calouste Gulbenkian Foundation

Hadley, Michael L (ed), 2001, *The Spiritual Roots of Restorative Justice*, New York: State University of New York Press

Harrington, Christine B, 1985, *Shadow Justice: The Ideology and Institutionalization of Alternatives to Court*, Westport, CT: Greenwood

Harris, M Kay, 1998, 'Reflections of a Skeptical Dreamer: Some Dilemmas in Restorative Justice Theory and Practice', *Contemporary Justice Review* 1: 57–70

Harvie, Christopher and Matthew, Colin, 2000, *Nineteenth-Century Britain: A Very Short Introduction*, Oxford: OUP

Hendriksen, Mike, 1995, *Restorative Justice in New Zealand: The Miracle Panacea or an Untenable Utopia?*, LLM Thesis, University of Auckland

Hinch, Ronald Owen, 1994, *Readings in Critical Criminology*, Scarborough, Ont: Prentice Hall Canada

Hofrichter, Richard, 1987, *Neighborhood Justice in Capitalist Society: The Expansion of the Informal State*, New York: Greenwood

Hoyle, Carolyn, 2002, 'Securing Justice for the "Non-Participating" Victim', in Hoyle, Carolyn and Young, Richard (eds), *New Visions of Crime Victims*, Oxford: Hart, pp 97–132

Hoyle, Carolyn and Young, Richard, 2002, 'Restorative Justice: Assessing the Prospects and Pitfalls', in McConville, Mike and Wilson, Geoffrey (eds), *The Handbook of Criminal Justice Process*, Oxford: OUP, pp 525–48

Hudson, Barbara, 2003, 'Victims and Offenders', in von Hirsch, Andrew, Roberts, Julian and Bottoms, Anthony (eds), *Restorative Justice and Criminal Justice: Competing or Reconcilable Paradigms*, Oxford: Hart, pp 177–94

John Howard Society of Alberta, 1997, *Restorative Justice*, Edmonton: John Howard Society

Johnstone, Gerry, 2002, *Restorative Justice: Ideas, Values, Debates*, Cullompton: Willan

Johnstone, Gerry (ed), 2003, *A Restorative Justice Reader*, Cullompton: Willan

Johnstone, Gerry, 2004, 'How, and in What Terms, Should Restorative Justice Be Conceived?', in Zehr, Howard and Toews, Barb (eds), *Critical Issues in Restorative Justice*, New York: Criminal Justice Press, pp 5–16

Karp, David and Walther, Lynne, 2001, 'Community Reparative Boards in Vermont', in Bazemore, Gordon and Schiff, Mara (eds), *Restorative Community Justice: Repairing Harm and Transforming Communities*, Cincinnati, OH: Anderson, pp 199–218

Kurki, Leena, 1999, *Incorporating Restorative and Community Justice into American Sentencing and Corrections*, Washington, DC: US Department of Justice, Office of Justice Programs, National Institute of Justice

Kurki, Leena, 2003, 'Evaluating Restorative Justice Practices', in von Hirsch, Andrew, Roberts, Julian and Bottoms, Anthony (eds), *Restorative Justice and Criminal Justice: Competing or Reconcilable Paradigms*, Oxford: Hart, pp 293–314

LaPrairie, Carol, 1998, 'The "New" Justice: Some Implications for Aboriginal Communities', *Canadian Journal of Criminology* 40: 61–79

Levinas, Emmanuel, 1998, *Ethics and Infinity: Conversations with Philippe Nemo*, Pittsburgh, PA: Dusquesne UP

Levrant, Sharon, Cullen, Francis T, Fulton, Betsy and Wozniak, John F, 1999, 'Reconsidering Restorative Justice: The Corruption of Benevolence Revisited?', *Crime and Delinquency* 45: 3–27

Llewellyn, Jennifer and Howse, Robert, 1998, *Restorative Justice: A Conceptual Framework*, Ottawa: Law Commission of Canada

Lyotard, Jean-François, 1984, *The Postmodern Condition: A Report on Knowledge*, Minneapolis, MN: University of Minnesota Press

Lyotard, Jean François and Thébaud, Jean-Loup, 1985, *Just Gaming*, Minneapolis, MN: University of Minnesota Press

MacIntyre, Alasdair, 1988, *Whose Justice? Which Rationality?*, South Bend, IN: Notre Dame UP

MacRae, Allan and Zehr, Howard, 2004, *The Little Book of Family Group Conference: New Zealand Style*, Intercourse, PA: Good Books

Marshall, Tony, 2003, 'Restorative Justice: An Overview', in Johnstone, Gerry (ed), *A Restorative Justice Reader: Texts, Sources, Context*, Cullompton: Willan, pp 21–28

Mathiesen, Thomas, 1998, 'Towards the 21st Century – Abolition, an Impossible Dream?', *Humanity and Society* 22: 4–22

Matthews, Roger (ed), 1988, *Informal Justice?*, London: Sage

Maxwell, Gabrielle and Morris, Allison, 1993, *Family, Victims and Culture: Youth Justice in New Zealand*, Wellington: Social Policy Agency/Institute of Criminology

McCold, Paul, 1998a, 'Restorative Justice: Variations on a Theme', in Walgrave, Lode (ed), *Restorative Justice for Juveniles: Potentialities, Risks, and Problems for Research*, Leuven: Leuven UP, pp 19–54

McCold, Paul (ed), 1998b, *Restorative Justice: An Annotated Bibliography*, New York: Criminal Justice Press

McCold, Paul, 2004, 'What is the Role of Community in Restorative Justice Theory and Practice?', in Zehr, Howard and Toews, Barb (eds), *Critical Issues in Restorative Justice*, New York: Criminal Justice Press, pp 155–72

McCold, Paul and Wachtel, Ted, 2002, 'Restorative Justice Theory Validation', in Weitekamp, Elmar and Kerner, Hans-Jürgen (eds), *Restorative Justice: Theoretical Foundations*, Cullompton: Willan, pp 110–42

McCold, Paul and Wachtel, Ted, 2003, 'Community is Not a Place: A New Look at Community Justice', in Johnstone, Gerry (ed), *A Restorative Justice Reader*, Cullompton: Willan, pp 294–303

McEvoy, Kieran and Newburn, Tim, 2003, *Criminology, Conflict Resolution, and Restorative Justice*, New York: Palgrave Macmillan

McLaughlin, Eugene, Fergusson, Ross, Hughes, Gordon and Westmarland, Louise (eds), 2003, *Restorative Justice: Critical Issues*, London: Sage (Open University)

Merry, Sally Engle and Milner, Neal A, 1993, *The Possibility of Popular Justice: A Case Study of Community Mediation in the United States*, Ann Arbor, MI: University of Michigan Press

Messmer, Heinz and Otto, Hans-Uwe, 1992, *Restorative Justice on Trial: Pitfalls and Potentials of Victim-Offender Mediation*, Boston, MA: Kluwer

Miers, David, 2004, 'Situating and Researching Restorative Justice in Great Britain', *Punishment and Society* 6: 23–46

Mika, Harry, 1995, 'On Limits and Needs: A Justice Agenda', *Mediation Quarterly* 12: 293–97

Milovanovic, Dragan, 2002, *Critical Criminology at the Edge: Postmodern Perspectives, Integration and Applications*, Westport, CT: Praeger

Moore, Dennis B and O'Connell, Terrance A, 2003, 'Family Conferencing in Wagga Wagga: A Communitarian Model of Justice', in Johnstone, Gerry (ed), *A Restorative Justice Reader*, Cullompton: Willan, pp 212–24

Morris, Allison and Young, Warren, 1987, *Juvenile Justice in New Zealand: Policy and Practice*, Wellington: Institute of Criminology, Victoria University of Wellington

Morris, Ruth, 1995, 'Not Enough!', *Mediation Quarterly* 12: 285–91

Morris, Ruth, 2000, *Stories of Transformative Justice*, Toronto: Canadian Scholars' Press

Nancy, Jean-Luc, 1991, *The Inoperative Community*, Minneapolis, MN: University of Minnesota Press

Nancy, Jean-Luc, 2000, *Being Singular Plural*, Stanford, CA: Stanford UP

New Zealand Ministry of Justice, 1995, *Restorative Justice: A Discussion Paper*, Wellington: Ministry of Justice

New Zealand Ministry of Justice, 1998, *Restorative Justice: The Public Submissions*, Wellington: Ministry of Justice

Olson, Susan and Dzur, Albert, 2004, 'Revisiting Informal Justice: Restorative Justice and Democratic Professionalism', *Law and Society Review* 38: 139–76

Pavlich, George, 1996a, *Justice Fragmented: Mediating Community Disputes under Postmodern Conditions*, London: Routledge

Pavlich, George, 1996b, 'The Power of Community Mediation: Government and Formation of Self', *Law and Society Review* 30: 101–27

Pavlich, George, 2000, *Critique and Radical Discourses on Crime*, Aldershot: Ashgate/Dartmouth

Pavlich, George, 2001, 'The Force of Community', in Braithwaite, John and Strang, Heather (eds), *Restorative Justice and Civil Society*, Cambridge: CUP, pp 56–68

Pavlich, George, 2002a, 'Towards an Ethics of Restorative Justice', in Walgrave, Lode (ed), *Restorative Justice and the Law*, Cullompton: Willan, pp 1–18

Pavlich, George, 2002b, 'Deconstructing Restoration: The Promise of Restorative Justice', in Weitekamp, Elmar and Kerner, Hans-Jürgen (eds), *Restorative Justice: Theoretical Foundations*, Cullompton: Willan, p 350

Pavlich, George, 2004, 'What are the Dangers as Well as the Promise of Restorative Justice?', in Zehr, Howard and Toews, Barb (eds), *Critical Issues in Restorative Justice*, New York: Criminal Justice Press, pp 173–84

Pavlich, George and Ratner, RS, 1996, '"Justice" and the Postmodern', in Peters, Michael, Marshall, Jim and Webster, Steve (eds), *Critical Theory, Poststructuralism and the Social Context*, Palmerston North, NZ: Dunmore, pp 143–59

Peachey, Dean, 2003, 'The Kitchener Experiment', in Johnstone, Gerry (ed), *A Restorative Justice Reader*, Cullompton: Willan, pp 178–86

Peachey, Dean and Tymec, Anne-Marie, 1989, *Membership Handbook*, The Network: Interaction for Conflict Resolution

Perry, John G, 2002, *Repairing Communities through Restorative Justice*, Lanham, MD: American Correctional Association

Pfohl, Stephen J, 1994, *Images of Deviance and Social Control: A Sociological History*, New York: McGraw-Hill

Pitzer, Donald E, 1997, *America's Communal Utopias*, Chapel Hill, NC: University of North Carolina Press

Pollard, Charles, 2001, 'If your Only Tool is a Hammer, all your Problems will Look Like Nails', in Strang, Heather and Braithwaite, John (eds), *Restorative Justice and Civil Society*, Cambridge: CUP, pp 165–79

Pranis, Kay, 2001, 'Restorative Justice, Social Justice and the Empowerment of Marginalized Populations', in Bazemore, Gordon and Schiff, Mara (eds), *Restorative Community Justice: Repairing Harm and Transforming Communities*, Cincinnati, OH: Anderson, pp 287–348

Pranis, Kay, 2003, *Peacemaking Circles: From Crime to Community*, St Paul, MN: Living Justice Press

Roberts, Simon, 1979, *Order and Dispute: An Introduction to Legal Anthropology*, New York: St Martin's Press

Roche, Declan, 2003, *Accountability in Restorative Justice*, Oxford: OUP

Rock, Paul, 1994, *Victimology*, Aldershot: Dartmouth

Rock, Paul, 2002, 'On Becoming a Victim', in Hoyle, Carolyn and Young, Richard (eds), *New Visions of Crime Victims*, Oxford: Hart, pp 1–22

Rose, Nikolas, 1999, *Powers of Freedom: Reframing Political Thought*, Cambridge: CUP de Sousa Santos, Boaventura, 1982, 'Law and Community: The Changing Nature of State Power in Later Capitalism', in Abel, Richard (ed), *The Politics of Informal Justice*, New York: Academic Press, pp 249–66

Schwartz, Martin D and Hatty, Suzanne, 2003, *Controversies in Critical Criminology*, Cincinnati, OH: Anderson

Selznick, Philip, 1998, 'Foundations of Communitarian Liberalism', in Etzioni, Amitai (ed), *The Essential Communitarian Reader*, Lanham, MD: Rowman & Littlefield, p 323

Sharpe, Susan, 1998, *Restorative Justice: A Vision for Healing and Change*, Edmonton: Edmonton Victim Offender Mediation Society

Sharpe, Susan, 2004, 'How Large Should the Restorative Justice "Tent" Be?', in Zehr, Howard and Toews, Barb (eds), *Critical Issues in Restorative Justice*, New York: Criminal Justice Press, pp 17–32

Shearing, Clifford, 2001, 'Transforming Security: A South African Experiment', in Strang, Heather and Braithwaite, John (eds), *Restorative Justice and Civil Society*, Cambridge: CUP, pp 14–34

Shonholtz, Raymond, 1978, 'Community Board Program', Mimeograph

Shonholtz, Raymond, 1984, 'Neighborhood Justice Systems: Work, Structure and Guiding Principles', *Mediation Quarterly* 5: 3–30

Shonholtz, Raymond, 1988/89, 'Community as Peacemaker: Making Neighborhood Justice Work', *Current Municipal Problems* 15: 291–330

Skeat, Walter W, 1993, *The Concise Dictionary of English Etymology*, Hertfordshire: Wadsworth

Smart, Barry, 1993, *Postmodernity*, London: Routledge

Strang, Heather, 2001, 'The Crime Victim Movement as a Force in Civil Society', in Strang, Heather and Braithwaite, John (eds), *Restorative Justice and Civil Society*, Cambridge: CUP, pp 69–82

Strang, Heather, 2002, *Repair or Revenge: Victims and Restorative Justice*, Oxford: OUP

Strang, Heather, 2003, 'Justice for Victims of Young Offenders: The Centrality of Emotional Harm and Restoration', in Johnstone, Gerry (ed), *A Restorative Justice Reader*, Cullompton: Willan, pp 286–93

Strang, Heather, 2004, 'Is Restorative Justice Imposing its Agenda on Victims?', in Zehr, Howard and Toews, Barb (eds), *Critical Issues in Restorative Justice*, New York: Criminal Justice Press, pp 95–106

Strang, Heather and Braithwaite, John, 2000, *Restorative Justice: Philosophy to Practice*, Burlington, VT: Ashgate

Strang, Heather and Braithwaite, John, 2001, *Restorative Justice and Civil Society*, Cambridge: CUP

Strang, Heather and Braithwaite, John, 2002, *Restorative Justice and Family Violence*, New York: CUP

Strickland, Ruth Ann, 2004, *Restorative Justice*, New York: Peter Lang

Stuart, Barry, 2001, 'Guiding Principles for Designing Peacemaking Circles', in Bazemore, Gordon and Schiff, Mara (eds), *Restorative Community Justice: Repairing Harm and Transforming Communities*, Cincinnati, OH: Anderson, pp 219–42

Sullivan, Dennis, Tifft, Larry and Cordella, Peter, 1998, 'The Phenomenon of Restorative Justice', *Contemporary Justice Review* 1: 1–14

Sullivan, Dennis and Tifft, Larry, 2001, *Restorative Justice: Healing the Foundations of Our Everyday Lives*, Monsey, NY: Willow Tree

Taylor, Ian R, 1999, *Crime in Context: A Critical Criminology of Market Societies*, Boulder, CO: Westview

Tomasic, Roman and Feeley, Malcolm (eds), 1982, *Neighborhood Justice: Assessment of an Emerging Idea*, New York: Longman

Torpey, John C, 2003, *Politics and the Past: On Repairing Historical Injustices*, Lanham, MD: Rowman & Littlefield

Umbreit, Mark, 1995, 'The Development and Impact of Victim-Offender Mediation in the United States', *Mediation Quarterly* 12: 263–76

Umbreit, Mark, 2001, *The Handbook of Victim Offender Mediation: An Essential Guide to Practice and Research*, San Francisco, CA: Jossey-Bass

Umbreit, Mark, Coates, Robert B and Kalanj, Boris, 1994, *Victim Meets Offender: The Impact of Restorative Justice and Mediation*, Monsey, NY: Criminal Justice Press

Umbreit, Mark and Greenwood, Jean, 2000, *National Survey of Victim-Offender Mediation Programs in the United States*, Washington, DC: US Department of Justice

Umbreit, Mark and Zehr, Howard, 1996, 'Restorative Family Group Conferences: Differing Models and Guidelines for Practice', *Federal Probation* 60: 24–29

Valier, Clive, 2002, *Theories of Crime and Punishment*, Harlow: Longman

Van Ness, Daniel, 1993, 'New Wine in Old Wineskins: Four Challenges of Restorative Justice', *Criminal Law Forum* 4: 251–76

Van Ness, Daniel and Strong, Karen, 2002, *Restoring Justice*, Cincinnati, OH: Anderson

von Hirsch, Andrew, Roberts, Julian and Bottoms, Anthony (eds), 2003, *Restorative Justice and Criminal Justice: Competing or Reconcilable Paradigms*, Oxford: Hart

Walgrave, Lode, 1994, 'Beyond Rehabilitation: In Search of a Constructive Alternative in the Judicial Response to Juvenile Crime', *European Journal on Criminal Policy and Research* 2: 57–75

Walgrave, Lode, 1995, 'Restorative Justice for Juveniles: Just a Technique or a Fully Fledged Alternative?', *Howard Journal of Criminal Justice* 34: 228–49

Walgrave, Lode (ed), 1998, *Restorative Justice for Juveniles: Potentialities, Risks, and Problems for Research*, Leuven: Leuven UP

Walgrave, Lode, 1999, 'Community Service as a Cornerstone of a Systematic Restorative Response to (Juvenile) Crime', in Bazemore, Gordon and Walgrave, Lode (eds), *Restorative Juvenile Justice: Repairing the Harm by Youth Crime*, New York: Criminal Justice Press

Walgrave, Lode, 2000, 'How Pure Can a Maximalist Approach to Restorative Justice Remain?', *Contemporary Justice Review* 3: 415–33

Walgrave, Lode, 2002a, 'From Community to Domination: In Search of Social Values for Restorative Justice', in Weitekamp, Elmar and Kerner, Hans-Jürgen (eds), *Restorative Justice: Theoretical Foundations*, Cullompton: Willan, pp 71–89

Walgrave, Lode (ed), 2002b, *Restorative Justice and the Law*, Portland, OR: Willan

Walgrave, Lode, 2003a, *Repositioning Restorative Justice*, Cullompton: Willan

Walgrave, Lode, 2003b, 'Imposing Restoration Instead of Inflicting Pain', in von Hirsch, Andrew, Roberts, Julian and Bottoms, Anthony (eds), *Restorative Justice and Criminal Justice: Competing or Reconcilable Paradigms*, Oxford: Hart, pp 61–78

Walgrave, Lode, 2004, 'Has Restorative Justice Appropriately Responded to Retribution Theory and Impulse?', in Zehr, Howard and Toews, Barb (eds), *Critical Issues in Restorative Justice*, New York: Criminal Justice Press, pp 47–60

Walklate, Sandra, 1989, *Victimology: The Victim and the Criminal Justice Process*, London: Unwin Hyman

Walters, Reece, 2003, *Deviant Knowledge: Criminology, Politics and Policy*, Cullompton: Willan

Walzer, Michael, 1983, *Spheres of Justice: A Defense of Pluralism*, New York: Basic Books

Weitekamp, Elmar, 2002, 'Restorative Justice: Present Prospects and Future Directions', in Weitekamp, Elmar and Kerner, Hans-Jürgen (eds), *Restorative Justice: Theoretical Foundations*, Cullompton: Willan, pp 308–21

Weitekamp, Elmar, 2003, 'The History of Restorative Justice', in Johnstone, Gerry (ed), *A Restorative Justice Reader*, Cullompton: Willan, pp 111–24

Weitekamp, Elmar and Kerner, Hans-Jürgen (eds), 2002, *Restorative Justice: Theoretical Foundations*, Cullompton: Willan

Woolford, Andrew and Ratner, RS, 2003, 'Nomadic Justice: Restorative Justice on the Margins of Law', *Social Justice* 30: 177–94

Wright, Martin, 1991, *Justice for Victims and Offenders: A Restorative Response to Crime*, Milton Keynes: Open UP

Wright, Martin, 2003, 'Justice without Lawyers: Enabling People to Resolve Their Conflicts', in Johnstone, Gerry (ed), *A Restorative Justice Reader*, Cullompton: Willan, pp 187–200

Young, Alison, 1996, *Imagining Crime: Textual Outlaws and Criminal Conversations*, London: Sage

Young, Iris M, 1990a, *Justice and the Politics of Difference*, Princeton, NJ: Princeton UP

Young, Iris M, 1990b, 'The Ideal of Community and the Politics of Difference', in Nicholson, Linda J (ed), *Feminism/ Postmodernism*, New York: Routledge, p 348

Zehr, Howard, 1990, *Changing Lenses: A New Focus for Crime and Justice*, Scottdale, PA: Herald

Zehr, Howard, 1995, 'Justice Paradigm Shift? Values and Visions in the Reform Process', *Mediation Quarterly* 12: 207–16

Zehr, Howard, 2002, *Fundamental Principles of Restorative Justice*, Intercourse, PA: Good Books

Zehr, Howard, 2003, 'Retributive Justice, Restorative Justice', in Johnstone, Gerry (ed), *A Restorative Justice Reader*, Cullompton: Willan, pp 69–82

Zehr, Howard and Mika, Harry, 1997, 'Fundamental Concepts of Restorative Justice', Akron, PA: Mennonite Central Committee

Zehr, Howard and Mika, Harry, 2002, 'Fundamental Principles of Restorative Justice', in Zehr, Howard (ed), *The Little Book of Restorative Justice*, Intercourse, PA: Good Books

Zehr, Howard and Toews, Barb (eds), 2004, *Critical Issues in Restorative Justice*, New York: Criminal Justice Press

Index

Access to justice
  movement 6
Adversarial legal system
  critique 5
Alternative dispute
  resolution 1
  rise of 6
Australia
  Wagga Wagga program 19

Barotse jurisprudence 6
Bentham 9
Biblical justice 26

Churches
  community justice 6
Communities
  aporia 95
  appeal 84
  care, of 87
  crime 97–98
  healing community
    harms 93–95
  ideal 83
  identification 101–02
  imitor paradox 95
  meaning of community 83,
                    86–88
  offenders and their 85–90
  ontological instabilities . .96–97
  open 102
  purposes of concept 85
  resources 89
  restorative visions of 90–93
  restoring 84–95
  secondary victim, as 85
  stakeholders 89
  state of restored 83–103
  strength 89

symbolic idea 88
universal 102
victims and 85–90,
                  98–103
Community development 4
Community justice 1, 86
  Canada 6
  churches 6
  New Zealand 6
  United States 5, 6
Community mediation
  processes 3–4
  United States 5
Community mediation
  and panels 2
Community of
  communities 7
Community panels
  United States 5
Community
  Relations Service 5
Community responsibility . .32–33
Courtroom justice
  restorative justice
    contrasted 2
Crime control
  culture 6
Criminal anthropology 66

Derrida 100–01,
              102, 115
Dream of purity 39
Durkheim 99

Enlightenment 65

Family group conferences . .2, 3
  agreement to participate 3
  aim 3
  co-ordination 3
  mediation techniques 3
  referees 3
  right relations,
    restoration of. 3
  structure 3
  youth justice 3

Foucault 8–11, 78

Frankfurt School 44

Free market regulation 7

Governmentality 8–11
  restorative
    governmentalities. 11–14

Harm 29–31, 114
  bearer of 80–82
  definition 30
  diagnosis 36–37
  healing the
    restorative way 31–34
  health 37–39
  imitor paradox and 34–36
  manifestations 30
  needs generated by 31

Heal .37

Health 37–39

Hume 65

Identity
  crime as violation of 37–38

***Imitor* paradox** 14–15, 20–23,
                    40, 81, 82,
                     100, 105
  communities 95
  implications 106–07
  key assumptions 116–17
  offender and 74–75
  political appeal of 107–08

Incorporation 105–06

Informal justice 1
  effect 7
  neo-Marxist critique 7–8
  net widening argument 8
  social welfare state and 7
  state control 7–8

Informal tribunals 2

Injustice 118

Just deserts 68

Justice 87
  biblical 26
  different traditions of . . .26–27
  ethics 41–42
  figurative images 1
  impartiality 1
  open-ended notion 115
  recalibrating ethically . .114–14
  restorative
    See Restorative justice and
      individual headings
  retributive 27
  traditions 26–27

Kant 65, 116

Legal anthropology 6

Lex talionis 2

Lombroso 66

Marx 99

Medical model 41

**Mennonite Central
  Committee** 6

**Methodological
  individualism** 99

Neighbourhood justice 1, 86
  United States 5, 6

New Zealand
  community justice 6
  restorative justice in 19
  youth justice 84

Offenders
  See also Responsible
    offenders
  accountability 69–74
  anthropology 66
  communal
    reintegration 69–74
  community and . .85–90, 98–103
  crime and 75–78

generator of
  contextual harms 68–69
harm, bearer of 80–82
identity reform 69–74
imitor paradox 74–75
indirect
  governance model 71
individual offender 78–79
meaning 68
perception of 65
political factors 73
punishment 65–67
restorative justice, in 67–74
treatment 65

**Poverty reduction
  strategies** 4

Punishment of offenders 2
  See also Offenders
  classic model 65
  purpose 66

Punishment regimes
  critique 5

Recidivism 5

**Reconciliation
  commissions** 2

Reintegrative shaming 72

Responsible offenders . . .65–82
  See also Offenders
  accountability 69–74
  communal
    reintegration 69–74
  identity reform 69–74
  restorative justice, in 67–74

Restorative justice 1
  abbreviated genealogy 4–8
  alternative values 27–28
  aporetic restorative
    values 21–22
  appendage to
    criminal justice, as 18–20
  approach 2
  appropriate governing . .13–14
  concepts upon
    which based 2
  courtroom justice
    contrasted 2
  definition 1–2
  dialogue 2
  focus 25

governing paradoxes . . .23–24
governmentalities 11–14
imitor paradox
  See Imitor paradox
impossible structure . . .108–09
independent
  alternative to
    criminal justice, as 16–17
  input of victims 2
  meaning 2, 26, 28
  parasitic healer 39–40
  parasitic identity 109–14
  participatory
    decision-making 2
  practices 2
  values 25, 29
  visions of harm 29–31
  what is governed 11
  what is restored by 37–39
  who governs 12–13
  who is governed 11–12

Sentencing circles 2

Shaming 32, 72

Social defence 4

State
  definition 8

Thames Valley program 19

Tiv justice 6

Transformative justice 33

United States
  community justice 5, 6
  community mediation 5
  community panels 5
  Community
    Relations Service 5
  neighbourhood justice 5, 6
  upliftment strategies 5
  victim-offender mediation . .19

Victim-offender mediation . .2, 53
  definition 53
  empowerment
    as a victim 59–60
  imitor paradox 57–59
  pre-mediation
    conference 55

preparing selected
  subjects to
  become victims 54–55
purpose 7
refusal 56–57
selection of cases 53–54
shaping victims
  through 55–56
United States 19

**Victim-sensitive
  mediation** 53

Victims **43–64**
centrality 43
communities and 85–90,
                                98–103
criminal justice
  approach 48
emphasis of
  restorative justice on. . 47–48,
                                73–74

impact statements 47
just implications 62–65
needs 46, 48–51
obligation to be a victim
  the restorative way. . . . 51–53
participation 47
restoring 46–51
support agencies 47
transcending
  victimhood 60–62

Vigilantism **118**

Wagga Wagga program **19**
Welfare society **7**

Youth justice **1**
family group conferences 3
New Zealand 84